BILLY GRAHAM

"I've had the honor of knowing both this book's author as well as its subject. Dr. Billy Graham led me to Christ in July of 1973. As I sat in my apartment in San Jose, California, Dr. Graham extended an invitation to receive Jesus as savior. The net was thrown, and I was caught. Over the years, I've been privileged to know and serve with Dr. Graham. He is a man of exceptional humility and spiritual power."

"In Terry Whalin's book, we glimpse Billy Graham the man as well as his ministry. These fifteen short but informative chapters paint a proper portrait of this extraordinary man of God. Terry's strength is his ability to capture Billy's life with poignant stories and providential incidences. I recommend the book and pray God would raise up more men and women dedicated to proclaiming the good news found in the Christ that Graham preached."

—Skip Heitzig, Pastor, Calvary Albuquerque

"Our polarized, divided world dearly misses the spirit of grace that Billy Graham brought to us. I'm very glad Terry Whalin has written a biography that introduces him anew."

—Philip Yancey, bestselling author of
What's So Amazing About Grace?"

"Well written and succinct, *Billy Graham* is an honest look at the man and his calling, his struggles to stay humble in the limelight, the difficulty of separation from his family, and his constant calling on God for the next step."

—Deborah Bedford, bestselling author of *His Other Wife*
and, with Joyce Meyer, *The Penny* and *Any Minute*

"Terry Whalin's love and respect for Billy Graham shows clearly in this riveting work. Yes, this is a story of one man's life and the team who supported him. It also clearly gives credit to the power of God's Spirit on whom Billy Graham relied to accomplish everything from *Christianity Today* to conferences for evangelists, a superb television and media ministry, and remarkable crusades around the world. I highly recommend this book, a book you will not want to put down. It will be a blessing to all who travel through its pages."

—**Tom Phillips**, Billy Graham Evangelistic Association
Vice President, Billy Graham Library

"Working with the Rev. Billy Graham on his memoir, *Just As I Am,* remains the highlight of my career. The story of the dairy farm boy who became the world's greatest evangelist and spiritual confidant to heads of state never grows old. **In** *Billy Graham, A Biography of America's Greatest Evangelist,* veteran author Terry Whalin offers a quick-reading account of Mr. Graham's life, jam-packed with anecdotes that bring him to life on the page. It's a fun and interesting read that promises to inspire and challenge you in your walk of faith.

—**Jerry B. Jenkins**, novelist and biographer

"Billy Graham has touched millions of lives with the Good News about Jesus. In this biography, my friend Terry Whalin has captured the remarkable story of how a boy from North Carolina took to the world stage and brought a message of hope to millions."

—**Suzanne Kuhn**, founder of SuzyQn4U and veteran retailer

"This book is very inspiring to me because I know both the author and the man whose life is being written about. Of course Billy Graham is well-known for his accomplishments, and for telling the world about God's love for mankind.

"For some, let me introduce my good friend Terry Whalin. Terry not only worked with Mr. Graham; he knew the humble and contrite man who preached the Gospel of Jesus to millions upon millions. I recommend not only the book as a story line but the author who shares Billy Graham's passion to touch lives for Jesus Christ."

—**Mike MacIntosh**, Pastor, Horizon Christian Fellowship

"Nothing will be more encouraging in your Christian life than to discover the sovereign work of God in the life of Billy Graham! Billy's story is your story and my story…what happens when the hand of God touches your life and leads you in the steps He has ordained for you! Every chapter reveals new vistas of God's grace in one life."

—**Glenna Salsbury**, Author of *Heavenly Treasures*
and *The Art of the Fresh Start*

BILLY GRAHAM

A Biography of America's
Greatest Evangelist

W. TERRY WHALIN

NEW YORK

BILLY GRAHAM
A Biography of America's Greatest Evangelist

Published in New York, New York, by Morgan James Publishing. Morgan James and The Entrepreneurial Publisher are trademarks of Morgan James, LLC. www.MorganJamesPublishing.com

The Morgan James Speakers Group can bring authors to your live event. For more information or to book an event visit The Morgan James Speakers Group at www.TheMorganJamesSpeakersGroup.com.

A free eBook edition is available with the purchase of this print book.

ISBN 978-1-63047-231-3 paperback
ISBN 978-1-63047-232-0 eBook
ISBN 978-1-63047-233-7 hardcover
Library of Congress Control Number: 2014937578

CLEARLY PRINT YOUR NAME ABOVE IN UPPER CASE

Instructions to claim your free eBook edition:
1. Download the BitLit app for Android or iOS
2. Write your name in **UPPER CASE** on the line
3. Use the BitLit app to submit a photo
4. Download your eBook to any device

Cover Design by:
Rachel Lopez
www.r2cdesign.com

Interior Design by:
Bonnie Bushman
bonnie@caboodlegraphics.com

In an effort to support local communities, raise awareness and funds, Morgan James Publishing donates a percentage of all book sales for the life of each book to Habitat for Humanity Peninsula and Greater Williamsburg.

Get involved today, visit
www.MorganJamesBuilds.com.

**Habitat
for Humanity®**
Peninsula and
Greater Williamsburg
Building Partner

Dedicated to the glory of God
and the life-changing power of Jesus Christ

To Christine,
who fills my life
with incredible joy.

TABLE OF CONTENTS

FOREWORD

By Luis Palau

I have always been fascinated with a good story. When I read about the lives of others, their experiences provide insights I can learn from but also follow for my own life. You hold in your hands the biography about one of the greatest mentors in my own life: Billy Graham.

When I was not even eighteen years old, I was lying on the living-room floor at my Uncle Arnold and Aunt Marjorie's home, listening to a short-wave HCJB radio program from Quito, Ecuador. I didn't hear the preacher's name, but I heard him exhorting and calling me to come to Jesus Christ in a vibrant, somewhat high-pitched, and excited voice. Later I realized I had been listening to Billy Graham. On that living-room floor, I prayed, "Jesus, someday use me on the radio to bring others to You, just as this program has firmed up my resolve to completely live for You." Little did I know that one day, by the grace of God, I would preach to tens of millions of people through radio and TV. The Lord has answered my youthful prayer more than I could have imagined.

Early in my Christian life, I lived in Cordoba, Argentina, and while attending a local church, I devoured biographies of several evangelists: Martin Luther, John Calvin, George Whitefield, John Wesley, D. L. Moody, Charles E. Finney, George Mueller, and Billy Sunday. These books influenced my life and ministry. Several years later in my early twenties, I began to hold street meetings and speak in little churches all over the country, yet my preaching seemed to have no power and few results. I gave God a deadline that if I didn't see converts by the end of the year, I would quit preaching. The end of the year came and went. My mind was made up. I didn't have the gift of evangelism.

On a Saturday morning, about four days into the new year, I bought a Spanish translation of Billy Graham's *The Secret of Happiness*. I was blessed reading Billy Graham's thoughts on the Beatitudes from Jesus's Sermon on the Mount in Matthew 5. I couldn't help but memorize the points Mr. Graham made on each Beatitude. That night I went to a Bible study where the speaker never showed up. Finally the man of the house said, "Luis, you're going to have to speak. None of the other preachers are here." I borrowed a Bible and repeated a few points I remembered from Billy Graham's book. Finally I reached the Beatitude, "Blessed are the pure in heart, for they shall see God"

(Matthew 5:8 RSV). Suddenly a woman from the neighborhood stood and cried out, "Somebody help me! My heart is not pure. How am I going to find God?" How delightful it was to lead her to Jesus Christ! What I learned that evening, of course, was something I had studied and should have known all along: the Holy Spirit does the convicting. I was just a vehicle. God used me in spite of myself, and He did it in His own good time. He had once again used Billy Graham's words to guide me and push me closer to Him.

Reports of Billy Graham's growing evangelistic ministry began to catch my eye. Friends gave me the book *Revival in Our Time*, which described Graham's 1949 Los Angeles crusade; the event that contributed to what Dr. J. Edwin Orr called the mid-century revival.

Missionaries lent me a dated copy of *Moody Monthly*'s report on Billy Graham's 1954 London crusade. What an impact that had on me! "Why can't we see this in our country?" I wanted to know. A whole nation could be turned around. Mass evangelism could lift a nation's moral and ethical standards. History bore that out. I began to dream that Argentina and eventually all of Latin America could be reached on a large scale for Jesus Christ. Eventually I came to America, met and married my wife, Patricia, and became an American citizen.

In July 1962, Pat and I worked as volunteers at the Billy Graham crusade in Fresno, California. I kept a thick notebook on every detail and learned the mechanics of mobilizing thousands of people. At a pre-crusade breakfast, we got to meet Billy Graham, and when he discovered my ambition was to preach in evangelistic crusades, he advised staying in the big cities. "Paul always went to the centers of population," he told us. "And Mr. Moody used to say that the cities were the mountains, and if you won the mountains, the valleys would take care of themselves."

If anyone wonders why our team's crusades have so closely resembled those of Billy Graham's over the years, they should have seen us eagerly absorbing the basics in Fresno. Through the years, I've had many opportunities to meet with Mr. Graham and learn from his example of how to touch the world for Christ. And although our model for citywide impact has begun to take on its own nuanced approach, the lessons learned from Billy Graham and his fabulous team have always run through my veins.

Before you dig into this book, I want to tell you about one more significant occasion. I was invited to be one of the speakers at the first International Conference for Itinerant Evangelists held in Amsterdam in 1983, which was sponsored by the Billy Graham Evangelistic Association. There were 4,000 delegates from 133 countries.

Billy Graham spoke on the opening night of the ten-day conference. The next evening, he asked me to speak on the sensitive subject of personal holiness. When I finished speaking, everyone in the audience got down on their knees on the convention floor and prayed in their own language, appealing to God for His cleansing power to make them a mighty force for evangelism around the world. Many wept. The effect was profound. I truly felt God's hand on the evening.

Ten days later, in his closing message, Billy shared from his heart, "This year, I will be sixty-five. At best, I don't have left more than a few years of this intensive evangelism that we engage in. Physically, it would be impossible. I have been engaged in it now over forty years. Three-fourths of my time is gone. At seventy-five I may still be able to hold some crusades, of course, but not on the scale we are doing now."

Here in the United States and abroad, journalists were asking, "Who is going to fill Billy's shoes once he's gone?" They are still wondering more than three decades later. But the answer should be rather obvious: *no one man.*

I have many stories of how Billy Graham impacted my life and ministry. No book can contain the stories of how his life in service to Jesus has changed the world. In this short biography, my friend Terry Whalin has captured the details of Billy Graham's beginnings on a farm in North Carolina, his call to the ministry and his service to America's leaders, and the global reach of his preaching around the world. As you read this book, I pray you will be moved to give your own life to Jesus and find inspiration to discover new ways to serve Him. For we all must remember the words of Galatians 2:20 – "I have been crucified with Christ and I no longer live, but Christ lives in me. The life I now live in the body, I live by faith in the Son of God, who loved me and gave himself for me."

Few exemplify that biblical reality better than the great Billy Graham.

Luis Palau and his ministry have shared the Gospel with more than one billion people through evangelistic events and media. He has spoken in person to thirty million people in seventy-five countries with more than 1 million registered decisions for Jesus Christ.

Chapter 1

EVANGELIST TO THE WORLD

C lutching his black Bible in one hand and a microphone in the other, Billy Graham stood outside in the howling wind in San Juan, Puerto Rico, near the Hiram Birthorn Stadium. The year was 1995. A satellite dish in the background was only one piece of a dazzling array of technology that had been assembled for one purpose—to proclaim the Good News of Jesus Christ.

The Billy Graham Evangelistic Association had worked for more than a year to coordinate the largest single evangelistic effort in the history of Christianity. That year, from March 16 through 18, Dr. Graham's preaching was transmitted from seventeen satellite pathways to thirty satellites across twenty-nine time zones for a total of 300 hours of transmission. His words were interpreted in forty-seven languages. Musical

1

clips and testimonies appropriate to various areas of the world were spliced into regional programs. For example, the Mandarin language version featured a testimony by tennis star Michael Chang and a Chinese Christian musical group. Thousands of venues around the globe were set up to receive the messages and project them on video screen. The settings ranged from a refugee camp in Rwanda to the rainforests of French Guiana. The largest hall in Burundi was packed out, with many looking in through the windows and doorways. In Cameroon, more than two thousand responded to the invitation to accept Christ. In Bangladesh, nearly 25 percent of the four thousand who attended gave their lives to Christ.

The numbers tabulated after the event were staggering:

- 185 countries reached
- messages heard in 117 languages
- 3,000 mission locations involved
- over 10 million seats occupied per night
- 1 to 1.5 million Christian workers trained in preparation
- over 500,000 prepared counselors
- 1 billion people viewed the broadcast in 117 countries
- another 3 billion attended video missions at various sites

At a satellite meeting in Kazakhstan, a student told her counselor, "I've tried everything, and now I turn to God as the last hope.... Something happened for which I've waited all my life."

Billy Graham has preached the Gospel message to more people in live audiences than anyone else in history—over 210 million people in more than 185 countries and territories. Hundreds of millions more have been reached through television, video, and film.

Spanning more than ninety years, Billy Graham's story cannot be contained in a single book. The stories of changed lives through his preaching could not be contained in a roomful of books. This short biography attempts to capture the key turning points in his life.

Several years ago, on his CNN program *Larry King Live*, Larry asked Billy Graham how he wanted to be remembered. Without a pause, Dr. Graham responded, "I want to be known as someone who was faithful. When I reach heaven, the Lord will respond, 'Well done, good and faithful servant. Enter into my rest.'"

Let's look at how Billy Graham has made this journey of faithfulness.

Chapter 2

NEAR THE CLEAN,
FRESH SMELL

Four days before the end of World War I, on November 7, 1918, Morrow Coffey Graham gave birth to a baby boy in a farmhouse near Charlotte, North Carolina. She named him William Franklin Graham, Jr. and called him Billy Frank.

The roots of the Graham family were deep in southern soil. Billy's two grandfathers, Ben Coffey and Crook Graham, fought in the Confederacy during the Civil War. As a result of wounds suffered during Pickett's Charge at Gettysburg, Coffee had only one leg and one eye, while Graham carried a Minié ball fired from a Yankee muzzle-loading rifle for the rest of his life.

Billy grew up on the family's three-hundred-acre dairy farm. Every day at three in the morning and again after school, he helped the hired hands milk seventy-five cows. The family chores left little time for idle play, but Billy had a reputation for being a bundle of energy, rushing from one activity to another.

One day his mother had had enough of his hyperactivity and hustled Billy Frank off to the doctor. In his office, she explained, "He never runs down, and it isn't normal. He's got way too much energy."

"Don't worry," the doctor said reassuringly. "It's the way he's built." The physician's words were almost prophetic.

As soon as Billy learned to read, his mother encouraged him to develop a habit of reading as much as he could. He was spellbound with the tales of Robin Hood in Sherwood Forest and the whole Tom Swift series. Among his favorite adventure stories were those of Tarzan. A new book was released every two months, and the young Graham could hardly wait for the next episode.

Billy often hung from the trees in his backyard and practiced his version of the Tarzan yell. It often frightened those driving horses down the road. Years later, his father would say, "I think all that yelling helped develop his voice."

One of his school bus drivers recalls another side of the youngster. Sometimes when Billy got off the bus with the other boys, he would reach underneath and turn the shutoff valve to the gas tank. The driver said, "I would go about a hundred yards and the engine would sputter out. I'd get out and shake my fist at him, but he'd only give me a laugh. It made him a hero to the other kids."

During his growing-up years, Billy learned the value of money, and his father taught him firsthand the importance of free enterprise. Every now and then when a calf was born on the farm, the elder Graham turned it over to Billy Frank and his friend Albert McMakin to be raised. When the calf reached the veal stage, the boys would market it and split the proceeds.

In general, the town newspaper was full of local stories, and radio was in its infancy. One day, William Graham, Sr. put together his first crystal radio set and located pioneer radio station KDKA in Pittsburgh. The family gathered around the squawking receiver and held their collective breath. For what seemed like a very long time, Mr. Graham turned three tuning dials to locate the station, and finally something intelligible broke through the static. Billy Frank and his siblings shouted, "That's it! We have it!"

A few years later, the Graham family was one of the first in the area to have a radio in their car. When his parents went into a store to shop, Billy Frank stretched across the backseat and listened to the mysterious distorted broadcast sounds. These wireless relays from Europe sounded like they were coming from a magical seashell. In particular, Graham was fascinated with the speaking style of a German named Adolf Hitler. While Billy Frank didn't understand his language, the intonation somewhat frightened him.

The barns on the family farm were roofed in tin, and on rainy days Billy loved to sneak sway into the hay barn and lie down on the sweet-smelling slipper piles of dried grass. He would listen and dream as the rain pounded the tin roof. The still and solitary sanctuary seemed to help shape his character. Even as an adult, when visiting a busy city, Graham would often find a quiet church where he could meditate in the cool, dim stillness.

There were plenty of animals on the farm, and from a young age, Billy learned to love dogs. The farm also had cats, and once, without knowing any better, Billy took a cat and shut it in a doghouse. While these animals hated each other by some ancient instinct, after spending the night together, they came out friends forever. The seeds of such an experience were planted in his heart. If bitter animal enemies could learn to work together, then people who were at odds with each other could also find ways to get along.

As a young boy, Billy had a close brush with death. When he was sick, his mother gave him what she thought was cough medicine but was actually iodine. Realizing her mistake immediately, she made a quick phone call to his Aunt Jennie, who suggested, "Give him some thick cream to neutralize the iodine." This remedy no doubt saved his life.

When Billy was nine years old, the dairy prospered enough that the Graham family was able to move into a larger, two-story, brick Colonial house that his father built for $9,000. The move meant a big change for Billy, his younger brother, Melvin, and his two sisters: no more baths in the washtub on the front porch—the family now had indoor plumbing. Billy Frank and Melvin shared a room that was sparsely furnished with twin beds and a white dresser.

The elder Graham had a reputation as an excellent horse trader, which carried over to his sale of cows. He often took

Billy along with him during these short trips. During one sales call at a farm about five miles away, Mr. Graham was explaining the excellent qualities of a particular animal when Billy Frank interrupted. "Daddy, that cow really kicks when you're milking her. She's very temperamental."

On the way home, Billy's father gave him some unforgettable instructions about not interrupting business negotiations.

Due to a shortage of cash and leisure time, Graham family outings were few and far between. But on an occasional Saturday night, the family would pile into the car and drive to the nearby country grocery store or sometimes even into Charlotte to Niven's Drugstore. On these special excursions, the treat was either an ice cream cone or a soft drink—but never both. Then, as the four children waited in the car with their mother, Mr. Graham would go into the barbershop for a shave.

Mother and Daddy Graham rarely went out for entertainment. But about once a year, they attended a potluck picnic at a community hall a mile away, which featured plenty of music. A favorite song of Mr. Graham's was "My Blue Heaven."

Sometimes the whole family went to see the movies. Some of the stars of the day were Will Rogers, Marie Dressler, and Wallace Beery. Nudity on the screen was rare at this time, but there were few restrictions. During a movie preview, a brief shot of a woman swimming in the nude flashed on the screen. Mrs. Graham grabbed Billy Frank's hand and commanded, "Close your eyes!"

The family always looked forward to spending two or three days each year on vacation. Usually they went to the beach, driving about eight hours to either Wilmington or

Myrtle Beach. After arriving, Mr. Graham would inquire at the various boardinghouses until he located the cheapest. Usually he managed to get a room and food for about a dollar a night per person.

Billy Frank's first long trip was to Washington, DC, four hundred miles from his home. His cousin Frank Black drove, but he wasn't interested in spending much time sightseeing because he had to get back home to his girlfriend. They went through the entire Smithsonian Institution—not the large complex of today—in forty minutes! On the same trip, they climbed every step of the Washington Monument.

Billy Frank's younger years were filled with experiences that made that time his happiest, even though when he was big enough, he had to help with some difficult family chores. The longest hours were spent in his mother's garden guiding the plow behind a mule to lay fertilizer down on the freshly sown seeds. Of course, the reward was that in the spring, summer, and fall, the Grahams enjoyed acres of corn, wheat, rye, and barley, and a variety of fresh vegetables.

When Billy's Big Ben alarm clock sounded at 2:30 a.m., he sometimes wanted to slam it on the floor and burrow back under the warm covers. But then he would hear the heavy footsteps in the hallway outside his upstairs bedroom, and he knew his father was up and expected his oldest son to hustle down the hill to wake up Pedro, one of the hired hands. Billy also knew that there would be no breakfast until all of the cows were milked. This was added incentive to get moving on the day.

Joe McCall, another one of the hired workers, usually called the cows into the barn: "Whoo-ee, whoo-ee, whoo-ee!" Instinctively, the cows headed to their stalls, where Billy Frank and the others fastened the stanchions around their necks. If a cow was particularly active, they also put kickers or restraining chains around their hind legs. Then Billy would set his three-legged stool and tin milk pail on the floor beneath the cow's working end. He'd press his head against her warm belly and begin working the udder "faucets" careful to keep out of the way of the swishing tail.

Billy repeated this process each morning in twenty stalls. And in the afternoon, after school, he milked the same twenty cows. The entire task took his flexible fingers about an hour and a half each time and translated into the commendable rate of five minutes per cow.

After the milking was done, Billy picked up a shovel and cleaned out the fresh manure from each stall, and with the help of the hired hands, he brought fresh hay from the hay barn next door to refill the feeding troughs.

One of Billy Frank's favorite rituals was carrying the five-gallon milk cans over to the milk-processing house. Before he was old enough to carry the heavy cans, he loved to watch the muscular men carry them down to the spring and set them into the clear water to cool. From there the milk was bottled and taken to town for delivery to homes.

Billy especially loved to watch Reese Brown, a black foreman on the farm for fifteen years. A few of the farmers were critical of the elder Graham because Reese was perhaps the highest paid farmhand in Mecklenburg County, earning three dollars a day.

But Reese was one of Mr. Graham's best friends. He had served with distinction in World War II as an army sergeant and was very intelligent. He was also one of the strongest men Billy Frank knew, with a great capacity for hard work. In the eyes of Billy, there wasn't anything that Reese didn't know or have the ability to do. If the young Graham did something Reese thought was wrong, he didn't hesitate to correct him. Almost like an uncle to him, Reese taught Billy to respect his father. Billy played often with Reese's children and enjoyed his wife's fabulous buttermilk biscuits in their tenant home.

After early morning chores, Billy Frank would head to the breakfast room at about five-thirty. Mrs. Graham chopped wood for the stove and cooked for the hungry men while they worked in the barns. With Billy's sister Catherine and the maid helping, Mrs. Graham served up grits, gravy, fresh eggs, ham or bacon, and hot homemade rolls. It was a traditional farm breakfast with all the milk they could drink.

After the hours of hard work, the fresh air of the dairy, and the good food, Billy Frank was ready for almost anything— except school. Some nights he got only three or four hours of sleep, and he often felt tired in the classroom. He contends the fatigue contributed to his poor grades. In elementary school, he made mostly As but in high school, he only had a C average.

Billy loved to read history, and also found he had a deep and abiding love for sports, especially baseball. One of the great thrills of his boyhood was shaking hands with Babe Ruth. In fact, Billy dreamed of becoming a professional baseball player someday, but wasn't quite good enough to continue in the sport. Ironically, Billy wasn't much aware of a professional baseball-player-turned-preacher named Billy Sunday, who was at the height of his ministry when Mr. Graham took his five-year-old son to hear him. Billy was overwhelmed with the huge crowd. He had no trouble being quiet, because his father had warned him that unless he was quiet during the service, the preacher would call out his name and have him arrested by the local police.

Throughout his school years, Billy dated several girls and enjoyed holding hands and kissing as much as any other young man. But he attributes his parents' strong love, discipline, and faith to keeping him on the straight and narrow. It never seemed right to him to have an intimate relationship with anyone except the woman he was married to.

Once during his senior year, he took part in an evening rehearsal of the school play. One of the girls in the cast coaxed Billy into a dark classroom. This particular girl had a reputation for making out with the boys. Before Billy realized what was happening, she was begging him to make love to her. His teenage hormones were as active as any other healthy young male's, but when this moment of temptation came, he silently cried out to God for strength and then darted from the classroom.

His sexual restraint wasn't for lack of knowledge. Like other teens, Billy discussed these appealing topics with other boys. He had the added tutor or one of the farm hands, Pedro. This older man was good-natured, but took the young Graham aside to confide in him about his sexual experiences with women.

It was Pedro who tried to teach Billy to chew tobacco. One day, Mr. Graham caught his oldest son with a chaw in his cheek, and that day became the last one that Pedro worked on the farm. Billy received a memorable thrashing from his father.

When it came to alcohol, Mr. Graham absolutely forbade it. He devised an unusual means to teach Billy Frank and his sister Catherine about the substance. Soon after the Prohibition Amendment, forbidding the sale of alcohol, was repealed, Mr. Graham brought home two bottles of beer and placed them in front of Billy Frank and Catherine in the kitchen. He handed a bottle to each of them and ordered, "Drink *all* of it." The shock of his unusual request turned them both against the bitter taste.

"From now on," Mr. Graham said, "whenever any of your friends try to get you to drink alcohol, just tell them that you've already tasted it, and you don't like it. That's all the reason you need to give." His approach worked, and Billy Frank never developed a taste for any alcoholic beverage.

Through consistent love and discipline, Billy learned to obey his mother and father without question. The concepts of lying, cheating, stealing, or destroying property were completely foreign to him. He also learned that laziness was one of the greatest evils, and he cherished the dignity and honor of hard work. Billy actually embraced with full abandon milking cows, cleaning out latrines, and shoveling manure, not because they were pleasant jobs but because sweat on one's brow held its own satisfaction.

Billy Frank was the oldest of the four Graham children, Catherine, Melvin and Jean. There were thirteen years between Billy Frank and Jean, his youngest sister. When Jean was three years old, Billy Frank carried her around on his shoulders. He walked from the living room to the dining room and accidentally dropped her onto the floor. Jean wasn't hurt, but for years in the family Billy Frank was teased about the incident.

Though his parents sometimes disagreed, and Billy could sense occasional tension between them, he never witnessed a word of profanity from either. They seemed to weather every problem and move on to what was important.

In the Graham home, the family Bible was read daily not as a ritual but as a practice established the day Billy's parents were married. The Bible was a cherished book, the very Word of God, and they sought God's help to keep the family united. Prayer was common in their home, and each time his parents prayed, Billy knew they were declaring their dependence on God for wisdom, strength, and courage—in spite of circumstances. The foundational prayer was that each of their children would come into the kingdom of God. It would be a few years before such prayer for Billy Frank would be answered.

Chapter 3

COMPLETELY CHANGED
IN A MOMENT

C hurch was always a part of the Graham's family life. They attended the Associate Reformed Presbyterian Church in downtown Charlotte. Billy can't remember a time when he didn't go to church. Even if he didn't feel like going, he never spoke it aloud to his parents because he knew "they would have whaled the tar out of me."

In 1934, Charlotte, North Carolina, had the reputation of being one of the leading churchgoing cities in the United States. At the invitation of many of the city churches, evangelist Dr. Mordecai Fowler Ham from Louisville, Kentucky, held a three-month-long revival meeting. The stately, balding man with a neatly trimmed white mustache and impeccable clothing preached every morning and every night except Mondays. This strong, rugged evangelist had a great knowledge of the Bible, and he didn't "soft pedal" sin. His candid denunciations of various evils were widely reported in the newspapers. To begin with, people were drawn to his meetings out of curiosity.

From the initial news that Dr. Ham was in town, Billy Frank decided not to attend the meetings. He felt negative about them—it sounded like a religious circus.

A number of Charlotte's ministers and several members of a group called the Christian Men's Club invited Dr. Ham to preach in a 5,000-seat tabernacle. The wooden building with a steel frame and sawdust ground cover was constructed especially for the meetings and located on the edge of town near the Cole Manufacturing Company.

Billy's parents were drawn to attend the meetings. Mrs. Graham went out of a desire to nurture her own spirituality but also to encourage growth in her husband. Later, Mr. Graham said, "My experience is that Dr. Ham's meetings opened my eyes to the truth." The Good News about Jesus took on fresh meaning to Mr. Graham and many others who attended.

Mrs. Graham was also deeply affected, and one day said, "I feel Dr. Ham's meetings did more, especially for the Christians, than any other meetings we've had here."

Despite his parents' enthusiasm, Billy Frank determined he didn't want to have anything to do with a person called an evangelist—particularly an evangelist with a colorful reputation like Dr. Ham's. Almost sixteen, he told his parents he would not go to hear the man.

Then one day early in the campaign, Billy read in the *Charlotte News* about one of Dr. Ham's sermons. He charged that immoral conditions existed at Central High School in Charlotte. Apparently, the evangelist knew what he was talking about and claimed to have affidavits from students. He contended a house across the street from the school was used for certain immoral escapades.

As the rumors flew, some students threatened to contest the accusations and demonstrate in front of the platform. Billy was curious about attending the meetings now, but wondered how he dared when he had resisted for almost a month. Then his friend, Albert McMakin, stepped in and suggested, "Why don't you come out and hear our fighting preacher?"

"Is he a fighter?" Billy asked. "I like a fighter."

That night Albert and Billy drove the Graham family vegetable truck to the crusade, loaded with people who wanted to attend. Everyone in their group sat in the back of the tabernacle. There were several thousand people in attendance, the largest crowd Billy had ever witnessed.

When Dr. Ham began, he opened his Bible and spoke straight from his text. His words resonated throughout the tabernacle, and though Billy Frank could not recall what Dr. Ham said, he was spellbound. The evangelist seemed to speak with the voice of the Holy Spirit.

That evening after the crusade, Billy Frank bumped along in the truck deep in thought. Later, stretched out on his bed at home, he stared out the window for a long time.

The next night nothing could stop Billy from attending Dr. Ham's crusade, and he became a faithful attendee night after night. He wasn't alone. Huge crowds were drawn to the tabernacle. Dr. Ham was a preacher who spoke on everyday topics like drinking, keeping the Sabbath, infidelity, and money. While Billy Frank had been in the church all his life, he couldn't recall a sermon about the Second Coming. Dr. Ham spoke of it often.

Neither had he heard a sermon about hell until these meetings. He knew people used the word for cursing, but Dr. Ham left no doubt that hell was a real place. He also told the people about the love of God in contrast to their sin and God's judgment. For the first time in his life, Billy Frank felt convicted about his own sinfulness—and he was confused.

How is it possible that the evangelist is talking to me? he wondered. He had been baptized as a baby, he could quote every word of the Shorter Catechism, and he had been confirmed in the Associate Reformed Presbyterian Church with the approval of the pastor and the elders. He was active in his church youth group and a diligent son. He got into mischief once in a while, but no more than any other teenager. Why did Billy Frank feel like Dr. Ham's pointing gestures struck right into his soul?

So convinced was he that Dr. Ham was speaking directly to him about sin and God's judgment if he didn't change his ways, one night he actually ducked behind the wide-brimmed hat of the lady in front of him. Yet despite his uncomfortable feelings, he was drawn irresistibly to the meetings.

Throughout these evenings, Billy struck up a friendship with Grady Wilson, who was already a Christian, but was having some convictions as well under Dr. Ham's preaching. Grady had an older brother, Thomas Walter, whom everyone called T.W. Billy Frank and Grady decided they could avoid Dr. Ham's pointed attacks if they joined the choir. Neither boy could sing, but they mouthed the words and held the hymnal. It seemed like the perfect evasion of Dr. Ham's stare.

Slowly it began to dawn on Billy that he did not have a personal relationship with Jesus Christ. He could not get into heaven because of his Christian parents. Each individual had to make a personal decision for Jesus.

One night around Billy's sixteenth birthday, Dr. Ham finished preaching and then gave an invitation for people to come forward and accept Christ. The audience sang all four verses of "Just As I Am," followed by "Almost Persuaded, Now to Believe." On the final verse of the second song, Billy Frank walked forward and stood in a small space in front of the platform. About three or four hundred people responded to the invitation that night.

On his way home, no bells sounded or signs flashed across the sky, but Billy felt a quiet peace. Before getting into bed, he got down on his knees for the first time and prayed, "Lord, I don't know what happened to me tonight. *You* know, and I thank you for the privilege."

In the spring of 1936, Billy Graham graduated from Sharon High School. His friend Albert McMakin, who invited him to hear Dr. Ham, was a field manager for the Fuller Brush Company. He invited Billy and his friends T.W. and Grady Wilson to hit the road and sell brushes. The job gave Billy the chance to earn some money for college in the fall as well as come face-to-face with the public as he went door-to-door selling brushes.

Before long, Graham outsold his friends with his approach. He would say to the housewife, "I haven't come here to sell you anything. I've come to give you a brush." This line of enticement never failed to get the housewife to want the free brush. But he always kept the free ones in the bottom of the case, so that he had to empty the other brushes onto a table to get to them. Upon seeing all the brushes, women would inevitably comment, "You know, I've never seen a brush quite like that one before." Or, "What is this one used for?" As soon as she began to ask about a product, Billy knew a sale was in progress. During the summer, he and his friends sold lots of brushes. They sent in their orders and received the brushes later in the mail. That required a return trip to the customers to deliver the brushes and to collect payment.

Sometimes a woman ordered a number of brushes and neglected to tell her husband. Billy learned that the best time to make a delivery was during suppertime or shortly thereafter, when both husband and wife were home. Then they could work out the situation and pay for the product. That summer, Billy learned a lot about human nature and honed his communication skills to convince a person to make a decision. It was a skill God would use in the days ahead.

Graham also developed another key skill—prayer. He prayed for opportunities to talk to people about Christ. Some customers complained to Albert, Billy's supervisor, that he sold Christ as much as he sold brushes. Nonetheless, his experiences as a salesman taught him some critical lessons for the future.

Chapter 4

COLLEGE: MORE THAN
AN EDUCATION

I n September 1936, the elder Graham drove his oldest son
and the Wilson brothers to Bob Jones College in Cleveland,
Tennessee. A sign on the dorm wall proclaimed, "Griping
Not Tolerated!" Those three words told a great deal about the
strict policies that awaited the three hundred students. During
a family Christmas trip to Florida, the Grahams learned about
Florida Bible Institute from a small ad in *Moody Monthly.*

While visiting Florida, Billy loved the warmer climate
and the palm trees. When they got back home, Graham was
supposed to go off to Bob Jones College for his second semester,
but his parents were praying and persisting in getting him
into Florida Bible Institute. He was overjoyed to learn of his
acceptance there.

Arriving in late January for the start of the semester, Billy thought Florida seemed like a paradise. The Institute was a Spanish-style country-club hotel with several outbuildings. Each building was clad in creamy pink stucco with tiled roofs and wrought-iron railings along red brick steps. The school was even smaller than Bob Jones. There were forty women and thirty men.

In the small-school atmosphere of the hotel, the students lived, dined, and studied. There was plenty of room for paying boarders as well. Often as many as fifty Christian ministers and laymen would spend the winter months at the Institute. The students served as the workforce—waiting tables, cooking, and washing dishes—at twenty cents an hour. Dr. Watson, the school president, was able to keep expenses down at the school by employing the students.

Billy preferred the outdoor chores. He drew his first outdoor assignment after serving the head table during the Christian Church denomination's conference. A man in a white suit gestured to make a point just as Billy was about to pour steaming hot coffee into his cup. When the man's arm hit the coffeepot, he exclaimed, knocking the pot out of Billy's hand and into the lap of a woman in a white dress. Soon both of them were hollering and demanding that Billy get away from their table. His waiting table days were numbered.

Graham liked his outdoor work—trimming the shrubs and cutting the lawns. The school was located beside a golf course, and Billy caddied for many famous preachers. These legendary figures came to the Institute to play golf and to speak in the chapel or for classes. In the process of walking around the fairway, carrying their golf bags and spotting their balls, Billy got to know these men, and some made an impression on him—usually positive, but sometimes negative.

The world-renowned evangelist, Gipsy Smith, who was in his seventies at the time, came to the Institute and stayed for weeks at a stretch. Because of his admiration for the man, Billy asked Smith for his autograph, and to his surprise, the evangelist turned him down. Graham was hurt by the rebuff, but later he became good friends with Smith and did get his autograph. Billy made a mental note to himself that if anyone was ever kind enough to ask for his autograph, he would gladly give it if at all possible.

The visiting faculty at the small school were not national figures in conservative Christian circles, but they were somewhat known and had a great deal of influence on the young Graham. Each of these preachers had a highly individual manner of speaking, coming from a variety of denominations. The experience broadened Billy's view of the body of Christ—trust wasn't limited to a single area of the church.

In the classroom, Graham heard a variety of different viewpoints, which provided an unusual blend of Christian thought ahead of its time. These teachers showed by example that people could come together in unity around the Bible and Jesus Christ rather than dwelling on a specific denomination or theology. The students were encouraged to think for themselves, yet always use the Bible as their authority and guide.

The atmosphere was very freeing for Graham, who had come with many questions. It made him feel he could interact with his professors and find answers. The Institute was committed to training every student as a witness for Jesus Christ—whether he went into full-time preaching or not. In pairs or as individuals, the students were sent to the local churches, missions, trailer parks, street corners, or jails to talk about their faith in Christ. If they didn't have sophistication, they made up for it with youthful enthusiasm. Graham spoke frequently at the trailer parks and at the Stockade, Tampa's jail.

While Billy Frank was in school in Florida, his family drove down from Charlotte, North Carolina to see him. The family stayed in a large rooming house that his aunt (his mother's sister) ran in Orlando. In the lobby of the rooming house, his father lifted Billy Frank's youngest sister Jean, age five and put her on a table. As Billy Frank, his parents, and some of the boarders watched, Jean preached a "sermon" saying, "If you don't accept Jesus, you are going straight to hell."

Reverend John Minder, a red-haired giant of a man from Switzerland, was the dean of men. He was an inspiration to Graham. Minder saw Billy as a spindly farm boy with lots of nail-biting energy, a mediocre academic record, and a zeal to serve Christ that exceeded his knowledge and skill.

Over the Easter weekend of 1937, Dr. Minder invited Billy to go with him to his summer conference grounds at Lake Swan in north Florida. On a blustery, cold Saturday, they met Cecil Underwood, a lay preacher who was pastoring the nearby Peniel Baptist Church. Mr. Underwood invited Dr. Minder to preach the following evening at a small Baptist church in Bostwick.

"No," he answered frankly, "Billy is going to preach."

Billy was stunned at the response of his professor. At the time he had four borrowed sermons that he had adapted and practiced but never preached to an audience. In the trailer parks or the Fellowship Club meetings in Charlotte, Graham simply ad-libbed. He knew it would be different preaching a real sermon at a Baptist church. *What will I do?* he thought to himself.

"Sir," Billy protested, "I've never preached a formal sermon in front of a church audience."

The two men laughed. "We'll pray for you," Mr. Underwood said, "and God will help you."

Reluctantly, Graham agreed. There was little else to do when the dean of his school offered his services. Billy was so frightened he spent almost the entire night studying and praying instead of sleeping. The next day, he practiced the sermons out loud, and by evening, he felt that at least one of the four should be twenty or thirty minutes in length.

A potbellied iron stove near the front of the tiny Bostwick Baptist Church took the chill off the room on the cold, windy night. The song leader, who was chewing tobacco, every so often walked to the door to spit. About forty ranchers and cowboys and their wives were crowded into the room.

Finally the moment arrived for Graham to step up to the pulpit. His knees were shaking, and perspiration glistened on his hands as he launched into his first sermon. In his mind, the first sermon finished almost as soon as it started, so he carried right on into the second sermon, then the third, and then the fourth. Finally, he sat down. Only eight minutes had passed!

When Billy returned to campus, he felt he had grown spiritually from the experience. At the same time, he felt a nagging tug on his heart. Was God calling him to preach the Gospel? If he had any glimmer of talent, it was hard for him or anyone else to find it at that time. He continued to practice his sermons. Many afternoons he paddled a canoe across Hillsborough Lake to a small island. Having only the alligators and birds for his congregation, he preached nonetheless—the loudness of his voice in direct contrast to the unresponsive nature of his audience.

Once some fishermen who drifted within earshot were amazed to hear such a bellowing voice emanate from such a beanpole of a lad. As he paddled the canoe back to school, his fellow students would often call out, "How many converts did you get today, Billy?"

Eighteen months after arriving at the Florida Bible Institute, Graham had started to exercise some of his spiritual gifts and to develop some preaching skills. He loved to tell people about Jesus Christ and how to find God's Good News of salvation. On Sundays, Billy often preached on the street corners of Tampa—sometimes five or six times a day. But his greatest place of ministry as a student was in the trailer parks. One of the largest in the county was known as the Tin Can Trailer Park. Two Christian women had received permission to hold religious services on Sunday evenings. They asked the young Graham to come and speak on a regular basis. The crowds ran anywhere from two hundred to one thousand. At the conclusion of the services, they took up a collection, which the ladies used for worthy projects, giving Graham five dollars to augment his small school budget.

A number of people confessed Jesus Christ as Lord in the trailer park. And it was there that Graham's teachers and fellow students affirmed his gift of preaching. He often wondered if he should preach for his life's work. In the late evenings, Graham walked the golf course beside the school and prayed. One night on the edge of the green, he got down on his knees, and then he lay prostrate on the ground and sobbed. "Oh, God, if you want me to serve you, I will."

As he stood in the moonlight and felt the gentle breeze on his face, everything looked the same, but in his heart, he had heard the still, small voice of God. The answer was *yes*. From that night in 1938, Billy Graham determined to be a preacher of the Gospel of Jesus Christ.

In early 1939, Woodrow Flynn, Graham's roommate, came to him and said, "I think you ought to be ordained. That would give you a standing in the Baptist Association and be of great benefit to you in many ways." As the two students talked and prayed about it, they agreed to get in touch with Cecil Underwood, who was still the pastor at Peniel Baptist Church. Reverend Underwood was happy to call together four or five neighboring pastors to form an ordination council.

The next Sunday morning, Billy preached at one of the churches and then went to Peniel for a two o'clock session. The little white frame church was hot inside, and Graham was nervous in front of the handful of rural Southern Baptist pastors, who took their ordination responsibilities very seriously. Under Pastor Underwood's direction, each pastor began to gently question Billy about his background and beliefs. One pastor decided to probe Graham's theological views. He must have decided that Billy was a Presbyterian turned Baptist and might have some incorrect theology. Finally, Graham's patience ran short and he said, "Brother, you've heard me preach around these parts and you've seen how the Lord has seen fit to bless. I'm not an expert on theology, but you know what I believe and how I preach, and that should be enough to satisfy you."

The pastor chuckled along with the others. The men approved Billy Graham for ordination, and the service was held that evening in the Peniel Baptist Church. Pastor Underwood presided, and Graham's roommate, Woodrow Flynn, preached the ordination sermon using the Bible passage, "Thou therefore endure hardness, as a good soldier of Jesus Christ" (2 Timothy 2:30 KJV).

On the platform in front of the small congregation, Billy knelt while half a dozen country preachers encircled him. He could feel their callused hands on his shoulders and on his head as they prayed him into this distinguished fellowship. Standing to his feet, he was now the Reverend Billy Graham, ordained Southern Baptist minister of the St. John's River Association.

During the summer of 1939, Billy held a two-week evangelistic meeting in Welaka Baptist Church. A fishing village on the St. John's River, Welaka had a reputation for being a tough place. But the Lord drew generous crowds to the nightly meetings, and during the invitations several people made commitments to Jesus Christ. Graham was developing his own preaching style and his own approach for giving the call to come to Christ.

That summer, Dr. John Minder gave his young protégé an incredible opportunity. He asked Graham to be his summer replacement at the large Tampa Gospel Tabernacle. For six weeks, Billy had his own church and carried out all the responsibilities of the pastor. He visited the members of the congregation and others in the neighborhood, inviting them to church. To his surprise, many of them came, listened, and responded.

In the Tampa hospitals, Billy prayed for the sick and held the hands of the dying. The lessons were invaluable for learning about the love and compassion a pastor must have for his people.

Every Sunday Billy preached, and every Saturday he entered an empty sanctuary and practiced out loud. Sometimes he had an audience of one—the janitor, who felt free to make suggestions. When Dr. Minder returned from his trip, he found his church in one piece so he appointed Billy his assistant pastor for his last year at Florida Bible Institute.

Billy graduated in May 1940, but during the following summer, God tugged his heart to continue his education at a liberal arts college. He went north and enrolled at Wheaton College.

Chapter 5

MORE EDUCATION, AND A MATE FOR LIFE

During Graham's final days as a student at the Florida Bible Institute, a Chicago attorney, Paul Fischer, stayed in the hotel section of the Institute with a business friend, Elner Edman, and Mr. Edman's mother. The two men had solid connections to a school just west of Chicago called Wheaton College. Paul's brother, Herman, was the chairman of the board for the college, and Elmer's brother, Ray, was a history professor and the interim president. The two businessmen heard Billy Graham preach at the Institute and encouraged him to further his education at Wheaton.

At the Institute, Billy had heard of Wheaton, and he knew Chicago and the suburbs were a whole different world from the South. He wondered if such a college would admit anyone from the Bible Institute, and also if he could survive the cold winters. To complicate matters further, Graham wondered if anyone would look at the poor grades he made in high school.

As Fischer and Edman talked with Billy, to his astonishment, Paul Fischer volunteered to pay his tuition at Wheaton for the first year, and Elner Edman said he would help with other expenses. With two influential references on his application, it appeared hopeful that he could study at Wheaton College.

With some anxiety and misgivings, Graham applied and was accepted. In September 1940, he drove to Wheaton to begin his study. The majority of his Florida Bible Institute credits did not transfer to Wheaton, so he began as a second-semester freshman.

Founded in 1860, Wheaton was a fully accredited college of liberal arts and sciences. The student population was integrated, and for the first time, Graham attended classes with blacks and others who came from Christian homes in most of the forty-eight states. While the school didn't call itself "fundamental," it had a strict code of conduct, which prohibited the staff and students from using tobacco and alcohol, playing cards, dancing, or joining any secret societies.

On one of Billy's first days at Wheaton, he was walking across campus when someone he didn't recognize greeted him, saying, "Hi, Bill, how's everything in North Carolina?"

The next day Billy learned that greeting came from the fourth president of the college, V. Raymond Edman. It was possible his brother had told Edman about Graham, but the young student was amazed that the president would know what he looked like and know his name.

Graham felt out of place and like a country hick on the Wheaton campus. The suburbs were a far cry from his life on the farm. During his first six weeks at Wheaton, he missed his old friends in the Sunshine State as well as his recent experiences of preaching. It made him wonder if he had made a mistake. At twenty-one, he was older than most of the students.

Another challenge to Billy's self-image was his out-of-style clothes and shoes. He decided to get some new clothing and tagged along with some students to Chicago's Maxwell Street, which was an open-air flea market. Mondays were bargain days. If a customer arrived early and was a sharp talker, he could purchase clothing for about a third of the asking price. For the grand sum of $4.95, Billy bought a beautiful turquoise tweed suit. In October, he wore it proudly to a football game, but out of the blue it began to rain. Soaking wet, his new pants shrunk to his ankles, and the seat of the pants became so tight they burst at the seams. He had to make a quick exit home to change. So much for a new suit of clothes.

Billy typically spoke in a rapid clip, and that together with his heavy southern accent made some think he was speaking a foreign language. At six feet two inches, he didn't exactly fade into the background.

The cold winter was a drastic change from the mild winters in Florida, and Billy thought he should at least try his hand (or feet) at ice-skating in nearby North Side Park. To put it succinctly, it was a disaster. After several spills, he gave up for good.

Graham was one of the few students on campus who owned a car. Before long, the Student Christian Council, which sent out student gospel teams to churches and missions on weekends, drafted Billy to participate. His first assignment was to drive a singing quartet to a church in Terre Haute, Indiana. He was to be the preacher. Graham leaped at the chance to deliver his first sermon since his arrival at Wheaton.

The quartet gave a glowing report to the council director about Billy's preaching. This garnered him a flood of speaking requests. At first, he turned most of them down, because he had committed himself to making his studies a high priority. And this commitment to academics showed with an 87 percent average at the end of the first quarter.

In downtown Wheaton, about a mile from the school, a church called United Gospel Tabernacle, or "the Tab," met on Sundays in the Masonic Lodge Hall. Dr. Ray Edman had pastored the church, but gave it up for his post as president of the college about the time Graham arrived at Wheaton. The congregation filled in with student preachers, and one Sunday, Billy was invited to speak.

After that, Graham received repeated invitations to speak at the Tab. The three hundred people packed into the hall on Sundays included professional people, businessmen, and college students—even college professors. In the summer of 1941, the Tab asked Graham to be their regular pastor when he returned to college in the fall. After much prayer and seeking the advice of his friend and counselor, Dr. Edman, Billy accepted the position.

Each week he prepared two sermons and led a prayer meeting on Wednesday nights. What Billy lacked in content, he made up for in volume of preaching. Unfortunately, to do this much preaching meant his college studies suffered. Soon his grades began to slip, and he struggled with the conflict.

On Sunday evening, December 7, 1941, someone told Billy that Pearl Harbor had been attacked. He didn't know where Pearl Harbor was located. Then a newsboy hawking copies of the *Chicago Tribune* made Billy aware that the United States was at war with Japan. His first thought was to volunteer. As an ordained Baptist minister, Billy felt like there had to be a place in the Chaplain Corps for him.

Immediately he wrote to the War Department to ask about the possibility. They responded that he would need to complete college and take a seminary course before he could enter the program. For the next three semesters, Graham's studies took on a renewed purpose, and the pastoral ministry to the members of the Tab's congregation deepened his preaching. Wheaton township turned its attention to matters of life and death. The war became a significant turning point for Billy Graham.

During his first semester at Wheaton, Billy met Johnny Streator, a fellow student who was working his way through college running a trucking service. After negotiating a price, Johnny would haul almost anything in his yellow pickup. He offered Billy an opportunity to work for fifty cents an hour. Graham took the job and spent many afternoons moving furniture and other items around the suburbs of western Chicago.

Serving in the navy before coming to Wheaton, Johnny was a little older than Billy and intended to go to China to serve on the mission field after he graduated from the college. While the pair rode around, Johnny mentioned a girl in the junior class—one of the most beautiful and dedicated girls he had ever met. Billy paid attention because the girl sounded like his type.

One afternoon Johnny and Billy were hanging around the front of Williston Hall, the girls' dorm, getting ready to haul some furniture for a woman in Glen Ellyn, the town next to Wheaton. Billy became conscious of his sweaty work clothes when Johnny let out a whoop and said, "Billy, here's the girl I was telling you about. It's Ruth Bell."

Graham stood a bit taller, and there looking right at him was a slender, hazel-eyed student as beautiful as Johnny had described her. Billy tried to say something, but it came out all wrong.

For the first seventeen years of her life, Ruth Bell grew up in Asia. Her father, Dr. L. Nelson Bell, was a medical missionary in the eastern Chinese providence of Kiangsu, and her family lived in the hospital compound. She grew up among loving parents and missionaries plus Chinese Christians, friends, and helpers. During her childhood, she was exposed to everything from sandstorms to monsoons to disease epidemics to bandit attacks to civil war. For her high school education, Ruth went to the Pyongyang Foreign School in Korea (now North Korea).

It took Billy a month to gather enough courage to ask Ruth for a date. For the Christmas holidays, the combined glee clubs at Wheaton were presenting Handel's *Messiah*. One day in the library, Billy spotted Ruth studying at one of the long tables. A couple of Graham's friends encouraged him to make his move right there. The librarian at the reference desk frowned as they whispered together.

Finally, Billy sauntered over to Ruth's table and scribbled a note proposing the concert date. To his surprise, she agreed. The next Sunday afternoon was cold and snowy. As Billy sat beside Ruth Bell in Pierce Chapel, he had a hard time paying attention to the music. Afterward, the couple walked over to a professor's house for some tea and conversation. Billy was immediately impressed that someone could be so attractive and yet so deeply spiritual at the same time.

Ruth told Billy that Saturday nights were dedicated to prayer and Bible study, in preparation for the Lord's day. It took creativity to date Ruth Bell. For example, on one date they took a long walk on a country road to a graveyard where they read tombstones. For Billy, such dates were a far cry from driving around Charlotte, North Carolina.

Billy realized he was smitten with Ruth Bell. It was love at first sight. Her missionary parents were Presbyterians, and since Graham had grown up in the Presbyterian denomination, it seemed like their relationship was a good fit. But there was a minor problem. Ruth was determined she was called to serve as a missionary to Tibet. Billy felt called to proclaim the Gospel of Jesus Christ, but without a specific geographic location.

Billy and Ruth spent a lot of time together on the campus and on simple dates, talking about the future.

One Sunday evening after church, Billy walked into the parlor of the home where he was rooming and collapsed in a chair. He was bemoaning the fact that he didn't stand a chance with Ruth because she was so poised and superior in her culture and intelligence. That evening he wrote home to his mother. "The reason I like Ruth so much is that she looks like you and reminds me of you."

By this time Billy had asked Ruth to marry him, but she was struggling with the decision. She continued to encourage Billy to keep an open mind about missionary service, even though she was beginning to realize that the Lord wasn't calling him in that direction.

Then one day Billy asked Ruth directly, "Do you believe God brought us together?"

"Without question," she said.

"In that case," Billy stated firmly, "God will lead me, and you'll do the following."

The exchange didn't get Billy a "yes" response, but he knew she was at least thinking it over.

An early test of the young couple's relationship came when Ruth's sister, Rosa, was diagnosed with tuberculosis. It was during the middle of Billy's second semester at Wheaton that Ruth dropped out of school to care for her sister. Rosa entered a hospital in New Mexico, and Ruth stayed with her through the next fall.

During the summer, Billy headed home and preached in several churches in the South. While he was in Florida, preaching in Dr. Minder's church, a thick envelope arrived from Ruth postmarked July 6, 1941. One of her first sentences made Billy shout with joy: "I'll marry you."

As Billy sat in his room, he read the letter over and over until church time. On page after page, Ruth explained how the Lord had worked in her heart, and now she felt that God wanted her to marry him.

Billy went to the church and preached his sermon. When he finished, the preacher turned to him and asked, "Do you know what you just said?"

"No," Graham confessed.

"I'm not sure the people did either," he replied.

In a few days Billy went on to another preaching series at Sharon Presbyterian Church in Charlotte. The congregation gave him an offering of $165. He rushed out and spent almost the entire amount on an engagement ring, which he described as having "a diamond so big you could almost see it with a magnifying glass."

At home, he showed off the ring and announced that he planned to present it to Ruth over in Montreat, North Carolina, that afternoon. Billy was told in no uncertain terms that the daytime hours were not romantic enough for such a gift.

That summer, Ruth was staying at the cottage of Buck Currie and his wife. Buck was the brother of Ed Currie, one of Ruth's father's fellow missionaries from China, and she affectionately called the couple aunt and uncle. Their house was built near a stream with swings that extended out over the water.

As Billy turned off the main road and drove in the direction of the Currie house, he saw a strange-looking woman walking toward him. She had long straight hair that stuck out every which way, and she wore a tattered, faded dress. Her feet were bare, and she had several teeth missing. Billy stared at the woman and drove right past her. Suddenly, it dawned on him that it was Ruth! She had blackened some of her teeth to fit the part of a backwoods mountain woman. He slammed on his brakes and backed up, and she climbed into his car, laughing.

When they arrived at the Currie home, Ruth shed her disguise, and they went for a long walk. As the sun began to sink in the west, they stood on what is now the Blue Ridge Parkway. The moon was rising on the other side of the mountain when Billy presented Ruth with the engagement ring and kissed her for the first time. He was convinced it had been a most romantic moment, but later Ruth confessed that she thought he was going to swallow her!

Back at the house, Ruth held the ring out to Billy and said, "I really can't wear this until I get permission from my parents."

The Bells were traveling, so Ruth sent them a telegram that read: "Billy has offered me a ring. May I wear it?"

Ruth's parents wired back, "Yes, if it fits."

Because Ruth had dropped out of college to care for her sister, when she returned to Wheaton, she was in the same class as Billy, and they would graduate together.

One day during his final semester at Wheaton, a Lincoln Continental pulled up outside the house where Billy was rooming. A young man emerged from the car and bounded up the steps to greet him as he came to the door.

"Hello, Mr. Graham. I'm Bob Van Kampen, the treasurer of the National Gideon Association. I'm here to sound you out about becoming the pastor of Western Springs Baptist Church, where I serve as a deacon." Graham was familiar with the church, located just twenty miles southeast of Wheaton. After talking with the young man for a while, he asked for a few weeks to pray about his decision.

The semester soon coming to a close, Billy began to feel the responsibility of his forthcoming marriage and support of a wife. He decided to accept the call to Western Springs Baptist, and would begin to pastor the church immediately following graduation.

There was one slight hitch, however. In his enthusiasm about the position, he neglected to tell his bride-to-be about it! When she found out, Ruth told Billy in no uncertain terms that she did not appreciate his insensitivity in not including her in such an important decision. Both agreed that the pastorate would probably be a temporary step in his ministry.

After their graduation in the spring, they began planning their wedding in earnest. They were married on Friday, August 13, 1943, at the Presbyterian conference center in Montreat, North Carolina. Ruth's parents, the Bells, had settled in Montreat after leaving China.

Following a short honeymoon in the resort town of Blowing Rock, North Carolina, the Grahams returned to the Chicago area and settled down to pastor Western Springs Baptist Church. The attendance grew steadily in spite of the fact that there were few Baptists in the area. Billy suggested to the elders that they change the name of the church to the Village Church, thereby encouraging the attendance of the greater numbers of Lutherans and Congregationalists living around them. The elders agreed to the change.

Driving down the street one day, a man headed in the opposite direction pulled alongside Billy's car.

"Excuse me. You're Billy Graham, aren't you?" he asked.

"Yes, sir."

"Glad to meet you. I'm Torrey Johnson."

"Oh, yes!" Billy said with enthusiasm. "I've heard you many times on the radio."

"I'd like to talk with you about some things," Torrey said. "I'll call you."

"Certainly, any time," Graham agreed.

Later Johnson reached Billy by phone and explained, "I've simply got too many things going right now. I have a large, growing church and my main radio program on Sunday afternoons. The ministry I'd like to pass on to someone else is a radio program called *Songs in the Night.* I've prayed about it and thought about it a lot lately, and I think you're the person who should have it."

Billy told Mr. Johnson that he would also have to pray about it and talk it over with the elders of his church.

"Of course," he said. "Call me as soon as you've made your decision."

Billy presented the idea to his board of elders and deacons. The radio time at WCFL in Chicago would cost $150 a week. The station was heard in the Midwest and into the South and East. It was a big decision, and one that Billy could not know would be one of the major turning points in his life.

At first, Ruth was not keen on the idea. From her perspective, the work at the Village Church was already demanding enough, and before long, they would be going off to the mission field. Initially, the church board rejected the idea of the radio program for lack of money. Then, the start-up funding was provided, and a quartet offered to sing before Billy's first radio message. The Lord seemed to be opening a door of opportunity.

Billy's first order of business was to get someone with a well-known name on the roster. No one had heard of him or his church. He considered the handsome bass baritone George Beverly Shea, who was a staff announcer at WMBI, the Moody Bible Institute radio station. Billy wondered if he could hire Shea to sing on his radio program.

With characteristic boldness, Billy headed to Moody and the radio station office on the top floor of the main building. Through the glass doors, he could see Shea in his office. The secretary said, "He's busy in a meeting."

Determined not to waste a trip to Chicago, Billy waited for his opportunity. When the door opened for a moment, he brushed past the secretary and said, "Mr. Shea, I'm sorry to intrude, but I have a quick proposal for you."

"Yes?"

"My name is Billy Graham, and I'm the pastor of the Village Church in Western Springs."

"I've heard of you," Shea acknowledged.

"Torrey Johnson has asked us to take over his Sunday night radio show, *Songs of the Night*," Billy said. He was speaking rapidly—too nervous to be flattered by Shea's recognition of his name. "And I'm convinced that the program would be most successful if you sang on it."

"Well, I don't know...." Shea hedged. Billy moved headlong into the conversation, outlining how well his singing would fit into the forty-five minute program. Admiring the persistence of the young preacher, and desiring to terminate the conversation, Shea agreed to try the program.

The Grahams scrambled to put together the first script for the new radio program. It consisted of a short story, three minutes in length, followed by a song. Billy decided to build his messages around current events. He would read the newspapers so that he could begin each message with something people had been hearing or reading about on that particular day.

The first broadcast put the church on the map. People began flocking to the Village Church to hear the broadcast live. Then the church began to receive letters from listeners throughout the Midwest. The program was to be supported by gifts from listeners as well as other backers, and this arrangement kept the budget in the black.

Besides the radio program, Billy conducted evangelistic meetings throughout the Midwest. Soon the elders of his church began expressing their growing discontentment with his lack of involvement in the local church.

At the same time, Torrey Johnson began a ministry in the Chicago area to reach young people and servicemen for Christ called Chicagoland Youth for Christ. He asked Billy to preach and to invite the young people to receive Christ at the close of the service. On the first Saturday night, May 27, 1944, the auditorium was full, and after the message, forty people came forward to receive Christ. The young preacher was humbled and encouraged by the eager response.

Youth for Christ (YFC) rallies began to spread across the Midwest to major cities such as Indianapolis, Detroit, and Philadelphia, and Billy was asked to speak at each one. His first plane trip was to the rally in Detroit.

As World War II was beginning to wind down, Billy was still hoping to serve as a chaplain. He had fulfilled the college requirement but had not completed a seminary chaplaincy course. He was commissioned as a second lieutenant in the army, but while awaiting his orders, Billy came down with a severe case of mumps and was in bed for six weeks. Ruth feared for his life as his temperature soared, and he became delirious.

Because of the illness, Billy could not begin his chaplaincy course at Harvard Divinity School. The Army chief of chaplains granted Graham a discharge, citing that the war was almost over. Billy also resigned as the pastor of the Village Church in Western Springs, and he became the first full-time evangelist for Youth for Christ.

The Lord was opening another chapter in his life.

Chapter 6

BEGINNING TO
TRAVEL FOR CHRIST

Toward the end of 1944, as Billy was recovering from the effects of his bout with the mumps, Torrey Johnson took him fishing off the Florida coast. Graham hoped for a relaxing, lazy day in the sun, but after they reached their spot, he could see the day would be much more than one of leisure.

For weeks Torrey Johnson had been burdened afresh with the idea of reaching young people for Christ. The early success of the evangelistic meetings of Chicagoland Youth for Christ had fueled a dream. The meetings had drawn large crowds of people, and Billy had been the first speaker in Orchestra Hall. Now as the two men sat fishing, Torrey began to talk with Billy about a blueprint for evangelism and Billy's part in it.

He wanted to organize youth rallies across the United States, Canada, and eventually the world and call the movement Youth for Christ International.

"I plan to ask Midwest Bible Church to allow me to work part time, and I will spend the rest of my time raising money for Youth for Christ International," Torrey said.

Almost immediately Billy could see the plan was from God. "But you'll need more money than you alone can raise," he said.

"I'll leave that to Bill Erny," Torrey stated with confidence. "He'll get it done." Erny was a businessman who knew about raising money. He had given Johnson some wise counsel and advice. Informally, Youth for Christ groups were already flourishing in Philadelphia, Indianapolis, Minneapolis, and New York City. Johnson planned to bring together twenty-five to fifty independent groups into a national organization.

The problem was lack of coordination between the various groups. Torrey said to Billy, "I believe you're the man to be our first full-time employee. Would you pray about becoming our national and international organizer?"

Billy couldn't hide his enthusiasm for the position, yet agreed to pray about it and talk it over with Ruth. In the end, the couple decided Billy should accept the job. Soon after he agreed to it, the invitations to preach began to pour in, and Billy began to travel around the Midwest to the various Youth for Christ rallies.

At one point, the young evangelist was boarding a train with his song leader, Al Smith, and someone handed him a telegram from Chicago. He put it in his pocket and didn't think about it again until hours later when he was on another train for Indianapolis. He opened the folded piece of paper and marveled at the news. Ruth was expecting their first child! Doctors had warned the couple that they might not be able to conceive children because of Billy's severe case of mumps. Surely God had intervened. Now more than ever they would have to make some key decisions about their lifestyle.

Working full time for Youth for Christ meant that Billy's travel schedule would increase, and Ruth didn't want to stay alone in Chicago during her pregnancy. Though they were more in love now than ever, the couple determined Ruth would be better off living near her parents in the little mountain community of Montreat, North Carolina. Her father practiced medicine in nearby Asheville. The Grahams felt the move was only a temporary one, but certainly a happy arrangement.

The military had priority on the use of all aircraft during the war, and Billy traveled largely by train or bus. The railroads issued clergy of all denominations half-price tickets, and Billy often took a bunk in a sleeping car and traveled during the night. As was typical of the early Youth for Christ meetings, Graham was introduced to the crowd of five thousand in Atlanta in late February 1945 as the director of the *Songs of the Night* broadcast in Chicago. The media reported that the new youth movement was active in three hundred cities.

During the first year in his new position, Billy Graham traveled coast to coast and to most of the provinces in Canada. He met with the local pastors and lay leaders and encouraged them to form committees to plan the rallies in advance. In addition to Youth for Christ rallies, Billy preached at other locations from Moody Church in Chicago to Princeton

Seminary in New Jersey. During the first part of her pregnancy, Ruth traveled with Billy to some of the meetings.

On September 21, 1945, Ruth walked her husband to the car. She didn't want Billy to make this particular trip. When the baby came, she wanted him by her side.

"Billy, the pains have already begun," she said.

Graham waved off his wife's concern as though he knew a great deal about babies. "No, I don't think so."

"Yes, they have," Ruth insisted. "The baby will be here soon!"

"Oh, it could take two or three weeks," Billy assured her, kissing her good-bye. Then he drove off to a speaking engagement in Mobile, Alabama. Later that evening, Virginia Leftwich Graham was born, the daughter the Grahams called Gigi.

In the spring of 1946, Torrey Johnson took a group of six men—including Billy—to Great Britain and Europe to launch Youth for Christ there. For most of the young men, it was their first trip overseas, and they flew in a military-type DC-4. On the trip across the United States, the plane was diverted to a U.S. airfield in Newfoundland. The social director at the base thought it was a small theater group and hastily arranged a late-night performance. Torrey neglected to tell the director that they were a Youth for Christ team.

The packed theater cheered and whistled as Charles "Chuck" Templeton, a pastor from Toronto, warmed up the crowd with his stories. They roared at Stratton Shufelt, the music director, when he sang "Shortnin' Bread." Next, Torrey appeared on the stage, and they began to yell, "Where are the girls? Show us the legs!"

Stratton sang another song, and it was received with boos. Backstage the group gathered for prayer while Billy went out and faced the crowd with an apology that they were not what the men had expected. Then he gave his testimony. The base commander was furious and wanted to throw the group in jail, but fortunately, relented so they could continue on to Europe.

Across Britain and Europe, various church leaders and pastors welcomed the YFC group. They stayed in people's homes or in inexpensive hotels. Then the team split into smaller groups, and Graham stayed with those in Great Britain. He spoke three or four times a day to capacity crowds. On a Saturday night, Billy might speak in a public hall followed by a fashionable church on Sunday morning. During the week, the venue might be a movie theater after the film showing. In the aftermath of World War II, people were hungry for hope and God's message.

Returning to the United States, Billy preached at half a dozen rallies from Toronto to San Antonio and from New Jersey to Oregon as well as at a couple of youth conferences. In the midst of his growing schedule, a Youth for Christ British leader, Gavin Hamilton, asked Graham to lead a series of campaigns in Britain. Billy felt his future was in this type of evangelism, but Torrey Johnson pointed out that it would cost a lot of money and that Graham would have to raise it himself.

Graham stepped out on a limb and asked Ruth to leave their one-year-old daughter with extended family in North Carolina and accompany him on the trip. She agreed to go. He wanted Stratton Shufelt to lead the music because he was well known in Britain, and asked him and his wife to join them.

Three weeks before the trip, Stratton called to say they couldn't leave their two little girls. So Billy turned to his friend's song leader, Cliff Barrows. Barrows along with his wife, Billie, said they would be thrilled to go. The Barrows and Graham headed first to England, and Ruth followed two months later. They had no timetable or any idea how long they would be traveling. The two couples formed a significant friendship on this trip and also significant roles on the team. Billie played the piano, Cliff led the singing, and Ruth prayed while Billy preached.

Every meeting brought a new experience. Halfway through Billy's sermon one evening to a packed out crowd in Reading, England, he heard a voice of protest coming from the middle of the church. The man who stood wore an ecclesiastical collar. "I don't believe a word of it!" he shouted to the crowd, claiming that Billy was teaching heresy.

Suddenly a woman in the balcony stood and carried on her own argument with the minister in the pew below. The minister's wife grabbed him by his coat and tried to pull him back into his seat. He continued to shout and struggled to free himself from his wife's grasp, but several ushers stepped forward and led him out of the church.

On another occasion at a local Baptist church, the team was pleased to see that the auditorium seated about one thousand. Then they learned that before the newly hired minister had started, morning attendance averaged nine and the evening attendance twenty! For the Youth for Christ rally, about one hundred people showed up, some of them responding to the invitation to make a decision for Christ.

After the couples had completed about fifty rallies across Great Britain, they felt tired and in need of a break. After a short flight, they arrived in Paris, France, and spent some time sightseeing. For Christmas, they planned to go to Nice, but without a word of warning from their travel agent, they were bumped to the Balmoral Hotel in Monte Carlo.

After two months away from her young daughter, Ruth returned to the United States, and Billy continued on with the Barrows for two more months of meetings. When Ruth arrived home, she was overjoyed to hear Gigi say, "Mama! Mama!" Then she learned that Gigi called any young woman "Mama" and any young man "Daddy."

Back in Europe, Billy began to worry about their dwindling finances. So he decided to write to the only wealthy man in America who he thought might give his request some consideration. He wrote to industrialist R. G. LeTourneau and honestly described their financial need for $7,000 to finish the tour. Two weeks later, a letter arrived with a cashier's check for the exact amount.

The team went on to Birmingham for a series of meetings, and LeTourneau himself came to one of them. He had built a factory nearby to produce earth-moving equipment, but apparently, it wasn't successful, and the industrialist had come to see the plant firsthand.

In April 1947, Billy returned home to his wife and daughter. He had been traveling for six months. The young couple had weathered a spiritual challenge during their separation. Billy's contact with church leaders in Great Britain had deepened his own spiritual life, and he had developed a renewed hunger for the Scriptures and a love for studying the Word of God. His preaching reflected this as he increased the frequency of quoting Scripture in his sermons.

At a Youth for Christ rally in Minneapolis that year, Billy was about to meet another man who would change the direction of his life. His first challenge, however, was getting to the rally. Billy was flying from Seattle to Minneapolis. He changed planes in Vancouver and boarded a Lockheed Lodestar in the pouring rain. When the plane took off, the fourteen passengers could see the beautiful Canadian Rockies in the moonlight. After a few hours, the plane was somewhere over Alberta when the flight attendant came down the aisle. Billy was the only passenger still awake, so she whispered to him, "We're having some difficulty."

"What is it?"

"All the airports within range of our fuel are shut down because of heavy snow," she explained.

"So we're going back to Vancouver?"

"We don't have enough fuel for that."

"What are we going to do?" he asked.

"That's what the pilot is trying to figure out now."

Billy began to feel nervous. Then the intercom crackled loudly enough to wake up all of the passengers. The pilot announced that he had located a radio tower and was communicating with the ground. They were telling him to land the plane as soon as possible because the storm was worsening. He understood there was an open field somewhere below. Locating a hole in the clouds, he began the descent.

"It's going to be bumpy," he warned. "We're going to have to use our own lights to see where we're going. It's a plowed field, but with the snow cover, I won't know which way the furrows are running. I'm going to leave the wheels up, and we'll slide in on the snow."

Then the flight attendant told the passengers to lean forward and tuck their heads between their knees. The pilot reassured them that because the plane was so low on fuel there would be no danger of fire.

The plane landed hard, sliding into the deep snow cover. Some passengers screamed as the aircraft came to an abrupt halt. Several suffered severe bruises from the seat belts, but no one was seriously injured. Billy had some bruises too, but overall was okay.

Because of the lateness of the hour and the fact that they were not near any roads, everyone spent the rest of the night on the plane. The pilot kept in touch by radio with a nearby small town. Officials there promised to send a wagon and team of horses at dawn to pick up the passengers and crew.

After loading into the wagon, they were taken to a waiting bus, which drove them into town. The airline put everyone up in a local boardinghouse. Billy was so exhausted from the experience that he collapsed into bed and fell asleep, even though it was already late morning.

An hour later, he awoke to the sound of loud knocking on his door. When he answered it, he was confronted with a Canadian Mountie.

"I need you to come with me," the Mountie said.

"Why is that?" Billy asked, incredulous.

"The man registered to this room last night is a bank robber. Until we can be sure who you are, you'll have to remain at the station with me." Fortunately, the pilot and the flight attendant were able to identify Graham as a fellow passenger.

After his long and harrowing experience, Billy eventually made it to Minneapolis and spoke as scheduled at Northwestern Schools. His invitation came from Dr. W. B. Riley, the evangelical leader and educator who had established Northwestern in 1902 as a response to the young people in his congregation.

During a private session with Dr. Riley, Billy was startled by the leader's declaration: "I believe you are God's man to replace me as president of Northwestern Schools." At this time, Billy didn't take the offer seriously because he was only in his late twenties, and Dr. Riley was in his mid-eighties. But the charismatic leader wanted someone young like Billy to instill a passion for Christ in young people.

As unsure as Billy felt about taking the responsibility, Dr. Riley insisted. Finally, Graham said, "Dr. Riley, I can't accept this responsibility. God hasn't shown it to me yet. But if it'll ease your mind, I could take it on an interim basis until the board can find a permanent president." Graham believed his call was to spread the Gospel. He could possibly further that cause through Christian education by training men and women to be passionate about spreading the Gospel. Nonetheless, he felt a deep uncertainty about the presidency of Northwestern.

In declining health, Dr. Riley presided over a board meeting at Northwestern on October 1, 1947. Billy was present and made a brief statement. "I have no clear indication from the Lord that I am to succeed Dr. Riley," he said. "God has called me to evangelism, and I have a definite responsibility and commitment to Youth for Christ at the present time. However, I would be glad to serve as interim president in the case of an emergency."

About two months later, Billy was at a Youth for Christ rally in Hattiesburg, Mississippi. One night at midnight, George Wilson, the business manager at Northwestern, telephoned to tell him that Dr. Riley had died. Graham's anthropology degree from Wheaton College didn't technically qualify him to lead the college, but he became the youngest college president in the nation only four years after his own graduation. Named interim president, Billy was instantly plunged into something that didn't interest him—running a school. He had a vision for Northwestern but no patience for it. Ruth remained in North Carolina with their two daughters. Anne was born in May 1948. With his travel schedule, Billy was on the road about a fourth of the time, and Ruth had no desire to move to Minneapolis. She kept reminding her husband that he was called to be an evangelist, not an educator.

The winds of change were blowing in Billy's life, and he could sense God directing his steps.

Chapter 7

INSIGHT INTO THE SCRIPTURES, AND THE MODESTO MANIFESTO

I n the mid-forties, Billy and his team used the term campaign for their meetings. Later, and to the present, they were called crusades. In October 1948, they were about to finish a two-and-a-half week campaign in Augusta, Georgia. On this Saturday night, an automobile dealer's convention was in a wild party mode in the room next to Billy's. Around one in the morning, Grady Wilson came to Graham's room and said, "I can't sleep."

Billy could relate. "I can't either, and tomorrow's a big day. I'm going over there and put a stop to this."

Pulling on a bathrobe, he went and pounded on the door for their attention. "Whaddya want?" groused the drunken man who opened the door.

"I want to speak to this crowd," Billy said. He brushed past the man and called for silence. The thirty or forty men and women, surprised at the appearance of a guest in a bathrobe, became quiet.

"I'm a minister of the Gospel," Graham began. They believed him, because in the Bible belt people can recognize an evangelist, even in a bathrobe! "I'm holding a revival campaign in this town. Some of you may have read about it in the newspaper." The revival had received some local media coverage, so his assumption was a safe one.

"I daresay most of you in this crowd are church members. Some of you are deacons and elders—maybe even Sunday school teachers. I know your pastors would be ashamed of you, because you're certainly not acting like Christians tonight." Then with even more boldness, he declared, "In fact, I *know* God is ashamed of you."

"That's right, preacher," one of them said. "I'm a deacon."

Then a woman confessed, "And I'm a Sunday school teacher."

Standing in the doorway, Billy preached a full evangelistic message to the awestruck crowd. He wasn't sure what happened after he left, but it was the end of the noise and commotion for the rest of the night.

In November 1948, the team headed to Modesto, California, for another campaign. Billy spoke in a large tent that had been specially erected for the event, but as it turned out, the tent wasn't large enough, because hundreds of people were turned away for lack of space.

During this period, the writer Sinclair Lewis had caricatured an evangelist called Elmer Gantry with some questionable practices. One afternoon during the Modesto meetings, Billy called together George Beverly Shea, Grady Wilson, and Cliff Barrows to discuss the potential problems of an evangelist and evangelistic meetings. Team members went to their rooms and jotted ideas and then returned in an hour to discuss them. In a short amount of time, they had created a complete list of commitments or resolutions that would guide their practices in the years to come.

The first issue was money. Nearly all evangelists, including Billy Graham, depended on offerings collected at the meetings. The temptation was to use strong emotional appeals to garner additional funds. Because there was little or no accountability for the funds, it was easy for an evangelist to abuse the system. The team decided to do everything they could to be accountable and to avoid financial abuses. They also decided to downplay the offering and depend on the local committee to raise as much money as possible beforehand.

Sexual morality was the next issue they tackled. Everyone knew evangelists were often separated from their families for long periods and could be tempted with immorality. The team pledged to avoid even the appearance of compromise. From that day forward, Billy never traveled alone, nor did he meet or eat alone with any woman other than his wife.

The third concern was the fact that evangelists often conducted their ministry apart from the local church. Some even openly criticized the local pastor and his work in their meetings. The team was convinced that such actions were not only counterproductive but against what the Bible taught. They pledged to support the local church publicly and avoid any anti-clergy attitudes.

The final issue was related to publicity. Many evangelists tended to exaggerate the number of attendees or converts at an event. The practice could lead people to disbelieve the work of the evangelist and his message. Billy and his team committed themselves to honesty and integrity in the reporting of any facts or figures related to the campaigns.

While these statements, which mirror the teaching of the Bible, may not seem profound, this Modesto Manifesto became the cornerstone of the operating principles for Billy Graham and his team in the years to come.

Several other series of meetings were held that year, and for the summer of 1949, the team prepared for a crusade in Los Angeles, the largest citywide meetings of its kind to date. At the end of August, before the campaign began, Billy attended the annual College Briefing Conference at Forest Home, becoming the youngest college president to speak at the conference.

Miss Henrietta Mears, a former high school chemistry teacher from Minneapolis, who had taken a respectable Sunday school program of 450 to an amazing attendance of 4,500, was now the director of religious education at First Presbyterian Church of Hollywood, and would chair the conference.

One night after the conference's evening session, Billy pondered a simple question: *Can I really trust the Bible?* He decided that if the answer was no, he could not with a clear conscience conduct the campaign in Los Angeles. At thirty years of age, it wasn't too late to quit the ministry and return to his wife in North Carolina. He wrestled with the answer.

Unable to sleep, he took a walk in the San Bernardino Mountains. Dropping to his knees in the moonlight, he placed his Bible on a tree stump. The moon didn't cast enough light for him to read its pages, but there at his makeshift altar, he prayed to God: "There are many things in this book that I don't understand," he began. "There are many problems with it for which I have no solution. There are many seeming contradictions, and many areas that do not correlate with modern science."

Billy was trying to be honest with God about his deepest thoughts and questions. Finally, he felt the assurance of the Holy Spirit, and he said, "Father, I am going to accept this as your Word—by faith. I'm going to allow faith to go beyond my intellectual questions and doubts, and I will believe this to be your inspired Word." Billy got to his feet and immediately sensed the presence of God and a new source of power within himself. While not every question was answered, he sensed that God was leading him, and he knew that he could depend on the Word.

However, as he walked back to his room, he continued to have a frightening lack of faith regarding the Los Angeles campaign. So much of the past year had been spent away from Ruth and his family because of his speaking engagements and work at Northwestern Schools. Of course, he had no way of knowing what was ahead in Los Angeles.

There was very little advance publicity for the Los Angeles crusade because the organizing committee, despite their efforts, couldn't get much cooperation from the local churches. A few days before the meetings began, Graham held his first press conference with a handful of reporters, but no stories about the conference appeared in the newspapers, much to the disappointment of Billy and the team.

The local committee struggled to raise the needed funds, their goal also being to broaden the number of churches involved. Billy's limited experience said that the more local churches were connected to the event, the better the follow-up afterward with new Christians. The committee also planned to erect a much larger tent than originally planned, because the crowds at evangelistic meetings seemed to grow as the event continued. This campaign was set to begin the last week of September and run for three weeks.

Just before opening night, Henrietta Mears arranged for Billy to speak to the Hollywood Christian Group, which included a number of well-known actors and actresses. That evening, Billy met Stuart Hamblen, a strong six-foot-two cowboy who was legendary on the West Coast for his popular two-hour radio show. Hamblen took a liking to Graham and promised to have him on his program.

The attendance at the early meetings averaged about three thousand each night and four thousand on Sunday afternoon, but the tent was never filled to capacity, even though since Billy's experience with God at Forest Home, he was preaching with renewed confidence and energy.

As promised, Stuart Hamblen invited Graham as a guest on his radio program. At first, Billy hesitated. He wondered if the Los Angeles campaign committee would want him to talk on a radio program sponsored by a tobacco company—and with Hamblen, the top radio personality on the West Coast. As Graham thought about the situation, he recalled how Jesus spent time with sinners and risked criticism from the religious leaders of his day. Billy decided to accept the invitation.

Hamblen surprised Billy when he encouraged his listeners to "go down to Billy Graham's tent and hear the preaching." Then he added, "I'll be there too!"

Later Billy learned that during the first night Stuart attended the meetings, he felt deeply convicted of his own sin and his need for Christ to save him. But because he didn't understand the spiritual battle going on, he became angry and stormed out of the meeting. He stayed away for two or three nights. When he returned, the angry feelings surfaced again, and he stormed out—actually shaking his fist at Billy as he left the tent.

The crowds grew. A week before the final meeting on Sunday, October 16, some of the committee members contended that Billy should extend the meetings. Others argued that the choir, the counselors, and the other workers were tired and that extending the meetings would be anticlimactic.

Billy, Cliff, Grady, and Bev (their nickname for George Beverly Shea) listened to the committee, but felt the need for specific direction. They decided to use Gideon's technique and put out a fleece. They would ask God for a definitive sign.

At four in the morning the next day, the telephone beside Billy's bed rang. In a voice punctuated with tears, Stuart

Hamblen begged to see Billy immediately. Grady and Wilma Wilson woke up to pray in another room with Ruth Graham.

By the time Billy was up and dressed, Stuart and his praying wife, Suzy, arrived at the hotel. The two men talked and prayed, and the rugged cowboy-turned-talk-show-host gave his life to Christ in simple faith. At the next service, Stuart Hamblen walked to the front of the tent in public declaration of his commitment to Christ. Almost immediately after the service, Stuart called his father, an old-fashioned Methodist preacher in West Texas. Billy heard the shout of joy over the line as Hamblen's father learned the news of his son's conversion. Later, Stuart would take his faith in Christ into his songwriting and write a song that is still heard today: "It Is No Secret [What God Can Do]."

They had their sign. Billy knew that God wanted them to extend the meetings in Los Angeles. But they wondered how long they should extend them. The team decided to ask the Lord for another clear indication or sign.

The next day when Billy arrived at the tent, the place was packed with reporters and photographers for the first time. During the previous three weeks, the press had taken almost no interest in the campaign. Billy inquired about the sudden interest. A reporter said, "You've just been kissed by William Randolph Hearst."

While Billy had heard of the famous newspaper owner, he had never met the man. The unsubstantiated story goes that Hearst called the editors with the order, "Puff Graham." Whether the story is true or not, the two Hearst newspapers, the *Los Angeles Examiner* and the *Los Angeles Herald Express*, both had front-page headline stories about the campaign. Also, the Hearst papers in New York, Chicago, Detroit, and San Francisco picked up the story. The next week, *Time* magazine wrote in the November 14, 1949, issue, "Blond, trumpet-lunged North Carolinian William Franklin Graham, Jr., a Southern Baptist minister who is also president of Northwestern Schools in Minneapolis, dominates his huge audience from the moment he strides onstage to the strains of 'Send a Great Revival in My Soul.' His lapel microphone, which gives added volume to his deep, cavernous voice, allows him to pace the platform as he talks, rising to his toes to drive home a point, clenching his fists, stabbing a finger at the sky, and straining to get his words to the furthermost corners of the tent."

The publicity helped the Los Angeles crusade gain greater public awareness and increased attendance. One evening near the close of the invitation, Billy particularly noticed a large man with tears rolling down his cheeks walking toward the front with his wife. While the evangelist didn't recognize the man, he asked Cliff Barrows to lead the audience in one more verse to give the couple time to reach the front. Reporters in the tent *did* recognize the tall man, and the next day's newspaper proclaimed, "Evangelist Converts Vaus, Sound Engineer in Vice Probe." Jim Vaus was the electronics wizard who had allegedly served as reputed mobster Mickey Cohen's personal wiretapper.

Several days after his conversion, Jim Vaus came to visit Billy Graham. He said, "Billy, I told Mickey Cohen what happened to me. Instead of getting angry, he said, 'Jim, I'm glad you did it. I hope you stick with it.'" Then Vaus told Billy about the contract on his life, apparently not from Cohen. His next words were, "Billy, would you be willing to talk to Mickey if I could arrange it?"

Without thinking about the implications, Graham shot back, "I'll go anywhere to talk to anyone about Christ."

They marked a meeting with the mobster, and one night Billy slipped out after the service and got away in Jim's car undetected. As they drove toward the house, Billy felt a bit uncertain, yet also genuine joy at the opportunity to tell the well-known mobster about Jesus. Arriving at an unimpressive home in an exclusive area called Brentwood, Billy noticed a parked car across the street with a man waiting inside.

As they entered the home, Billy was taken aback at Cohen's short stature. The mobster's brown eyes were curious, and he invited them in. "What'll you have to drink?" he asked.

"I'll have a Coca-Cola," Graham said.

"That's great," he said. "I think I'll have one, too." Apparently alone, Cohen served the drinks.

After settling in the living room, Jim Vaus told his testimony of how he had found new life in Christ and how he now had peace and joy in his heart. Then, in simple terms, Billy explained the Gospel of Christ. He prayed in his heart for the right words—just as he did when he spoke to the large gatherings in the tent.

Mickey responded thoughtfully to the talk with some facts about his own life, specifically how he regularly supported charitable organizations. He added that although his religious belief was different from Billy's, he respected the evangelist and Jim Vaus's decision. The men had a brief prayer before they left.

The next day, to Billy's surprise, a local newspaper blared, "Wiretapper In Confession As Evangelist Tries To Save Cohen." Without Graham's knowledge or approval, the visit had been leaked to the press; maybe it was the man watching Cohen's home, someone involved in the campaign, or perhaps Cohen himself. Later, Cohen denied the validity of the story, saying, "I think the whole thing is a publicity stunt, and that's what I'm trying to avoid—publicity. I don't want to meet the guy. I haven't got time."

These sorts of reports by the media surprised Billy, but he decided not to be concerned or discouraged by them.

The campaign moved into its fifth week, and seating was rearranged to accommodate 3,000 more chairs. When these additional seats were filled, they added an extension to the tent, doubling its size. The news media attended every meeting, and the reports in the press were more positive.

One member of the clergy took a leave of absence from his pastorate so he could serve as night watchman at the tent after the meetings. He slept under the platform to keep an eye on the place. One night he heard the chain rattling at the entrance.

He called out, "Who goes there?"

"Just me," came the reply.

"What do you want?"

"I just want to find Jesus."

The pastor let the man inside and led him to a personal faith in Christ.

Billy and the team wondered if they should extend the crusade for a sixth week. It was difficult to know if they should continue without using numerical success as their standard for finding the will of God.

During the daytime hours, Billy spent his time in sermon preparation and prayer. He sought the Lord's direction for his preaching as well as other ministry opportunities.

Under the leadership of Lutheran spiritual leader Armin Gesswein, prayer meetings were organized across Southern California. Besides students, businessmen, and families, a group of forty to fifty women prayed each day. These women sat directly in front of the platform each night with expectant faith that God would work in the hearts of the people who heard the Word.

The team had no staff to handle all the phone calls, letters, and telegrams. At the end of the sixth week, the young evangelist didn't even seek God about whether he should continue. He knew he was drained and often felt too weak to even stand at the pulpit. Sometimes he paced the platform to keep himself from falling over. The meetings had taken their toll: Billy had lost weight, and he had dark circles around his eyes. The other members of the team also felt the pressure on their families. None would leave the tent until every person who desired it had been personally counseled.

In spite of the exhaustion, Graham somehow learned to lean on God's grace and strength and pressed on for two more weeks. As the eighth week approached, they all knew it would be the last. Louis Zamperini, the U. S. track star who pulled down a Nazi swastika flag in the 1936 Olympics and was a hero during World War II, come to Christ that last week. Unhappy and broken in spirit, he had wandered into the meeting, accepted Christ, and his life was transformed.

On Sunday afternoon, November 20, 1949, eleven thousand people packed the tent with standing room only. Thousands milled around in the street unable to get inside, and hundreds left because they couldn't hear. On the platform, 450 ministers sat with Billy Graham. To these clergy fell the responsibility of guiding the people who had made decisions for Christ during the eight weeks. Thousands of people responded to Billy's sixty-five full sermons and hundreds of evangelistic talks to small groups. God had answered prayer in an amazing fashion and touched many lives, changing them forever.

Chapter 8

FOUNDATIONS
FOR THE FUTURE

A fter the close of the meetings in Los Angeles, the team wondered about the future. Was the Los Angeles crusade to be a historic event, or was it the beginning of a pattern? Only time would tell.

The city of Boston, with its reputation for being the cultural and educational capital of the U.S., was their next target. Somewhat intimidated by the city's reputation, Billy felt the opportunity was a gift from God. The press coverage was extensive, and the meetings were extended to seventeen days, more than doubling their original schedule. The final event was held at the 13,000-seat Boston Garden with unprecedented crowds, requiring that some people were turned away.

The team was encouraged during the campaign with the response of Roman Catholics. They recognized that the Lord was opening doors in hearts and even in universities for their return to New England with a follow-up series of meetings.

During the summer of 1950, Billy felt torn between his evangelistic calling and his duties as president of Northwestern Schools. Out of deep conviction, he resigned the position, but the board of directors wouldn't accept his resignation. He continued to seek God about the presidency, and finally, in February 1952, he tried again to resign, and the board accepted his resignation.

In the late winter of 1950, Graham and his team held their first major southern crusade in Columbia, South Carolina. The meetings were well received and attended by dignitaries such as Governor Strom Thurmond, who later became the longest-serving member of the Senate. More important, the team grew to include people like Willis Haymaker, who helped them with organization and widening their circles of church participation to include Roman Catholic as well as Protestant churches. Tedd Smith joined the team as the pianist and Billy's administrative assistant.

In March of that year, the young evangelist began an intensive twenty-day series of meetings, which took the team to fifteen cities, most of them one-night rallies. What a work of God in this tour of New England! Thousands attended, and hundreds made commitments to Christ. Often the weather was bitter cold or rainy, yet overflow crowds packed surrounding streets. Also, for the first time, the team arranged a series of meetings with university students, and the experiences convinced Billy of the power of the Holy Spirit among these young minds.

The team selected the Boston Common for the closing meeting, and people were expected to come from all over New England. Billy wondered if there would be enough people to have a "respectable" attendance. On the Sunday morning of the final session, it was pouring rain. Graham gathered the team in his hotel room and said, "Let's pray and ask God to clear the sky." After the prayer, Billy's anxiety was calmed and his heart filled with peace.

At noon, the newspapers called to see if the meeting would be cancelled because of the weather. Billy told the press, "No, the sun will be shining by the time the preaching begins at three o'clock." Laughter was the general response from the journalists. Even his friends laughed at the suggestion that the sun would shine for the meetings.

As the first hymn was being sung at two o'clock, the rain stopped. An hour later, Billy walked to the pulpit and addressed a crowed of fifty thousand people.

One of the key experiences for Billy during this Boston meeting was when he met John Bolten, the German industrialist who immigrated to Boston in 1929 and recommitted his life to Christ during these meetings.

One day, John mentioned something to Billy that touched him in an area where he felt most vulnerable. Despite the success in Los Angeles and the current crusade in Boston, Graham wondered if his ministry was simply a flash success, or something that would stand the test of time. While a part of Billy felt at home in evangelism, he found the nationwide publicity unnerving, and at times, he wanted to escape to a different occupation.

As they walked across the Boston Common, John said to him, "Billy, I can envision you preaching in the great stadiums of the capital cities of the world. I believe the world is ripe and ready to listen to a voice of authority like yours. They are in need of the Gospel. You are the man to give it to them." Graham was humbled by the visionary words from this friend, and he listened to his sage advice whenever he spoke.

In early July 1950, about three hundred churches invited the Billy Graham team to hold a crusade in Portland, Oregon. One of the key men in this event was Dr. Frank Phillips, a veterinarian whom Billy had met during a Youth for Christ rally in 1948. Dr. Phillips directed the Portland crusade. A temporary tabernacle was constructed that held twelve thousand people. Overall, more than five hundred thousand attended the six-week crusade, and about nine thousand signed decision cards for Christ.

This crusade marked the first time some special needs in the audience were considered. Dr. Phillips made arrangements for a local pastor to sign for the deaf. They also held separate meetings for men and women to talk about problems in the American home. About eleven thousand men attended the first meeting and were told not to tell their wives the contents of the meeting. Out of curiosity, about thirty thousand women packed the tabernacle and surrounding area for the women's session. Many parents attended the meetings, and satellite tents were set up complete with cribs for the care of three hundred babies and young children. For the final session, the governors of Oregon and Washington both attended, including an estimated crowd of twenty-two thousand, with twelve hundred coming forward at the invitation.

The numbers never tell the full story of a crusade. God touches individuals at each meeting, but the statistics were verification of the increasing responsiveness to Billy Graham's evangelistic ministry. It showed him in a vivid fashion that the Holy Spirit was moving in America.

Another door for ministry opened for Billy Graham as a part of the Portland crusade. Bob Pierce told Billy about a filmmaker named Dick Ross who had prepared a well-received documentary. "You ought to ask him to film one of your crusades," Bob suggested.

After some discussion, the local committee invited Dick to make a color film about the crusade to be shown in churches throughout the Northwest. Ross's production company was called Great Commission Films, and eventually it merged with the company the team had set up called Billy Graham Films. Later, they changed the name to World Wide Pictures, because Billy felt his name might keep some people from attending. World Wide Pictures built their studios across the street from Walt Disney Studios in Burbank, California. *The Portland Story* was the first of more than two hundred films produced there. Thousands have come to Christ through films produced by World Wide Pictures.

Several months before the Portland crusade, while in Boston, Billy heard on the radio that Dr. Walter A. Maier, the Lutheran theologian and radio preacher, had died of a heart attack. The news jolted Graham, and he immediately knelt in his hotel room and asked God to raise up someone to take Dr. Maier's place on the radio. While TV was in its infancy, radio was the predominant communication vehicle, and only a few evangelical radio programs were available nationally.

Early that summer as Billy was preaching at a conference in New Jersey, Cliff Barrows and Billy stopped for lunch at a roadside diner. Suddenly, they were greeted by a big, smiling man who pumped Billy's hand and said, "Hallelujah! What an answer to prayer! I was just sitting here praying that I might meet Billy Graham, and in you walk! I didn't even know you were on the East Coast."

Cliff and Billy were meeting Dr. Theodore Elsner, a minister from Philadelphia. "I have a great burden on my heart," he said. "It's a message that I believe is from the Lord. Billy, you must go on national radio. You know Dr. Maier is dead, and you're the man God could use to touch America through radio." Then, Dr. Elsner urged Billy to contact his son-in-law, Fred Dienert, who with his partner, Walter Bennett, was a radio agent. Billy graciously thanked Dr. Elsner, but didn't take any immediate action because of his intense schedule.

A few weeks later, Billy was speaking at a Michigan conference when he met two well-dressed men: Walter Bennett and Fred Dienert. Their mission was to get Billy interested in a national radio program. While Graham appreciated their concern, he told them that he was president of Northwestern Schools in Minneapolis and obviously active in evangelism so his schedule wouldn't allow any more activity. His closest advisors agreed with his decision.

Now at the Portland crusade, these two persistent men laid an ambush to meet with Billy for another session. They claimed to need only five minutes of his time, but Graham was so irritated that he often took the back elevator to avoid them.

One night when Billy walked out of the hotel, the two men were standing outside, and one of them said, "We wanted to say good-bye. We're leaving tonight for Chicago."

Billy laughed. "All right, fellows, if before midnight tonight I should get twenty-five thousand dollars for the purpose of a radio broadcast, I'll take that as an answer to prayer and be willing to do a national broadcast." The thought struck the two men as ridiculous; they shared a laugh with Billy and left for their flight home.

That night, more than seventeen thousand attended the meeting. Just before Billy introduced his guest, Bob Pierce, to tell about his trip to the Far East, Graham mentioned the burden of Bennett and Dienert for a national radio broadcast. Billy also mentioned the $25,000 condition that he laid down, and the audience laughed with Graham at the idea.

After the meeting and the invitation, several people dropped by to greet Billy and to say that God had spoken to them about the radio ministry. They left checks, cash, and pledges. Billy could not believe it.

When everyone had left, Frank Phillips said, "Billy, people have given us twenty-four thousand dollars tonight for a radio broadcast!"

Their confidence and generosity was almost enough to make Billy weep. How could this be God's answer and be $1,000 short? The team went out to dinner and returned to their hotel at about eleven-thirty. When they passed the desk, the clerk said, "Mr. Graham, there are two letters for you."

The letters were postmarked two days earlier and were from two businessmen that Billy hardly knew. They wrote to say they believed Billy should go on the air, and each had enclosed a check for $500—it was the missing $1,000!

Stunned, Billy bowed his head and thanked God in silent prayer. As he turned to the elevator, he saw Walter Bennett and Fred Dienert standing in the lobby. The men had gone to the airport, but believed the Lord was telling them not to go on to Chicago just yet.

With a hand on the shoulder of each man, Billy said, "Sign us up for the radio for at least thirteen weeks. God has answered our prayer, and we will take the $25,000 as a step of faith."

The actual cost was substantially beyond the amount collected—$7,000 per week to be exact, for a total of $91,000—but the men took the step of faith. Walter and Fred arrived in New York to meet with ABC, but they could find only a junior executive to help them. He informed the men that the ABC board had decided not to allow any more religious programming on the network.

Fred and Walter protested strongly, saying, "You promised it. We've guaranteed this young man, Billy Graham, that he has a network. To change your minds now is very unfair. Get a hold of the board."

"That's impossible," the junior executive said. "They're all playing golf."

"Well, get a-hold of them on the golf course."

The executive countered, "I can't do that. You'll have to wait until Monday."

The men responded, "We're not coming back on Monday. We'll sit here until this is resolved."

Seeing that Walter and Fred would not be deterred, the ABC executive finally reached a board member on the eighteenth hole and explained the situation. On the spot, the board reversed their decision, and *The Hour of Decision* radio program, which continues today, was scheduled for broadcast.

Billy's new effort to raise money for radio evangelism created a problem. Underneath Grady Wilson's bed in a Portland hotel, the Graham team was holding $25,000 in cash, checks, and pledges in a shoebox.

The problem was that, in the past, the local committee collected all funds from a campaign or crusade and deposited them in a local bank account established for the meetings. The money in the shoebox had nothing to do with the crusade. It was earmarked for radio ministry. Thus, it could not be deposited in the local account. Neither Wilson nor Graham wanted to open a bank account under his own name, because they would be subject to income tax on the full amount.

The current money problem pointed to a larger problem: there was no formal organization. Known simply as the Graham-Barrows Campaigns, the team had never formed a separate corporation or opened a bank account for the organization. There was no board of directors. Now with the new radio program, Billy knew that people would be sending them funds for radio time, and they could be dealing with a large number of people and even larger amounts of money. In the past, they had talked about establishing a separate organization for the evangelistic work. Now was perhaps the time.

While in Portland, Billy called George Wilson, the business manager at Northwestern Schools. George suggested they move ahead with formal incorporation. Almost immediately, he filed documents in St. Paul, the capital of Minnesota, which established the Billy Graham Evangelistic Association (BGEA). Billy strongly protested the name choice. Just as strongly, George contended that the organization needed to be identified with Billy Graham, since he was the major evangelist. Graham has often wished his name wasn't so visible, because he knows the organization belongs to God and not him. He has often said, "If we ever lose sight of this fact [that the organization belongs to God], God will withdraw his blessing from our work."

The incorporation papers required a statement of purpose, and Wilson included the following, which still holds true today: "To spread and propagate the Gospel of the Lord Jesus Christ by any and all … means." The first directors were Billy Graham, Cliff Barrows, Grady Wilson, and George Wilson, with the later addition of George Beverly Shea.

George Wilson rented some office space across the street from Northwestern Schools, and soon resigned from the school to become BGEA's full-time business manager. In a simple, unglamorous fashion, the BGEA offices remained in Minneapolis, Minnesota for many years. In 2001, BGEA announced the headquarters would be moved to Charlotte, North Carolina, the city where Billy Graham was born. Three years later in 2004, the Billy Graham Evangelistic Association opened the newly built headquarters on Billy Graham Parkway in Charlotte.

Chapter 9

MEETING THE PRESIDENT, AND FAMILY PRIVACY

W hile Billy and the team were at the 1950 Portland crusade, he met Abraham Vereide, a businessman who was already having regular prayer groups with other businessmen in the Seattle area.

A year later, when they held a crusade in Seattle, Vereide came every night, and before or after each meeting, he talked with Billy about his burden to reach political leaders for Christ. Abraham wanted to begin an annual presidential prayer breakfast. Graham encouraged his friend, and as his plans became firm, he promised to talk with President Dwight D. Eisenhower about it.

Billy was concerned about the follow-up after his evangelistic meetings, and he prayed for someone who knew something about this matter. Dawson Trotman, the founder and leader of the Navigators ministry, arrived to help with follow-up after the 1951 Seattle crusade. Trotman took the lead in developing follow-up methods that later became a significant part of the Graham ministry. After each meeting, team members like Billy, Cliff Barrows, and others became nearly exhausted counseling the people who came forward. Finally Dawson went to Billy and said, "Don't you believe that God has given us gifts, too? Your gift is platform preaching. Let us handle the counseling of those who come forward." This experience taught Billy a great lesson: to recognize the gifts of God in others and to delegate responsibility to them.

Billy had met General Eisenhower at the headquarters in 1952 when Eisenhower was Supreme Commander of Allied Forces in Europe. Billy had talked about his faith privately with the general and promised him that their discussions would remain private and not public. That meeting was the first of many between the two men.

That same year General Eisenhower ran for the presidency of the United States and won. As soon as he became president, he proclaimed a National Day of Prayer and joined the National Presbyterian Church. Billy approached Eisenhower about a presidential prayer breakfast, but the president was extremely reluctant about the idea. However, he did promise to think about it. Eventually he called or wrote Senator Frank Carlson and said that he would attend the first breakfast, but would not promise to attend any subsequent ones so that he didn't set a precedent.

During a meeting in Denver, President Eisenhower introduced Graham to the hotel magnate Conrad Hilton, who became a financial sponsor of the annual Presidential Prayer Breakfasts in Washington for several years. The driving force behind these breakfasts was Abraham Vereide, then Senate Chaplain Dr. Richard Halverson, and then Doug Coe. During the first fifteen Presidential Prayer Breakfasts, Billy Graham brought the main address and used the platform as an opportunity to preach the Gospel and even to give a clear invitation to follow Christ.

In formal settings such as the Oval Office, Eisenhower met with Billy Graham, but they also enjoyed some rounds of golf together. One day Billy watched the president jump with glee when his partner, Grady Wilson, sank a fifty-foot putt in Palm Springs, California. The putt clinched their victory over Billy and his partner. Golf has often given Billy a means to relax in an informal setting with well-known people. Because of his time with President Eisenhower, Billy gained a growing admiration for his character, the intensity of his faith, and how he applied that faith to his policies and programs. That faith was severely tested with physical illnesses, including heart and stroke problems.

Late one Sunday night in August 1955, Billy was awakened in a Washington hotel room. Sid Richardson told Billy, "I've had a terrible time tracking you down. The president wants to see you, and the White House couldn't locate you. I'll let them know where you are." A bit later, the White House called and told him that a car would take him the next morning to the president's farm in Gettysburg. Billy had no idea what the president wanted and prayed for wisdom to have the right words.

When Graham arrived at the property, to his surprise, President Eisenhower opened the car door. At first, the visit looked like an ordinary social occasion. The pair had a quiet lunch and then went upstairs to pray with Mamie, the First Lady, who was sick in bed. Then the president asked Billy if he would like to tour the famous Gettysburg battlefield.

"Both of my grandfathers fought in that battle," Billy said.

"Do you know which group they were with—North or South Carolina?"

Unsure, Billy telephoned his mother, who told him the name of the company that his grandfather, Ben Coffey, had been part of. Eisenhower took Billy to the location where he thought that company might have engaged in battle in Pickett's Charge.

At the battlefield, they switched from a car to a golf cart, with the Secret Service following behind in another cart. The president narrated as he drove around the battlefield. Because he was a student of the Civil War, and especially Gettysburg, he gave Billy a great deal of new information.

When the men returned to his house and stood in his den, the president paced in front of his fireplace. Billy sensed that he was about to learn the real reason for his visit.

"Do you believe in heaven?" the president asked.

"Yes, sir, I do."

"Give me your reasons."

Reaching into his pocket, Billy pulled out his New Testament and gave the president a guided tour through the Scriptures about a Christian's future in heaven.

"How can a person know that he's going to heaven?" Eisenhower asked.

As Graham explained the Gospel, he sensed that the president was reassured with the message: salvation is by grace through Jesus Christ alone, not by anything that an individual does in his or her own strength.

The day was coming to a close, and Billy told the president that he had to speak in Charlotte, North Carolina, that evening. He was not going to make his Washington plane if he didn't call.

"You can fly straight to Charlotte in my Aero Commander," the president offered. Billy accepted, and he arrived in time for his evening talk.

In early 1952, Billy and the team held a five-week crusade in Washington, DC. Because of an unprecedented act of Congress, he held a service on the Capitol steps on Sunday, February 3. Speaker of the House Sam Rayburn gave the final authorization, saying, "This country needs a revival, and I believe Billy Graham is bringing it to us."

Thousands stood in the rain to hear the thirty-four-year-old evangelist. During the weeks of the crusade, Billy often visited the various members of Congress. That's where he made friends with Senators Richard M. Nixon and Lyndon B. Johnson.

In 1953, Billy's friend John Bolten was with the team during a series of meetings in the Dallas Cotton Bowl. One evening, Billy sensed that his preaching didn't seem to have the spiritual depth or power that he had felt in other meetings, even though a number of people came forward at the invitation. After the meeting, John and Billy took a walk together and had a serious conversation.

John confronted Billy. "I've noticed you don't speak about the Cross. How can anyone be converted without having at least one view of the Cross—where our Lord died for us? You must preach the Cross of Christ. You must remind people of the blood that was shed there. The Bible speaks of no greater power than the power of the Cross."

At first, Graham resisted the confrontation. More often than not, his sermons emphasized the importance and meaning of the Cross. The night Billy couldn't sleep and, before morning, he knew that John was right. He made a commitment never to preach again without making certain that the Gospel was complete and made as clear as possible, centering on Christ's sacrificial death for our sins on the Cross and His resurrection from the dead for our salvation.

As Billy's popularity and visibility increased, the curiosity seekers descended on his small town of Montreat, North Carolina. Tucked in a valley of the beautiful Blue Ridge Mountains, these visitors were determined to see the Graham home. They trampled through Ruth's flowerbeds and peered in the windows at all hours.

By bus and car, tourists invaded the town, parading up and down the streets around the Graham home. While they meant no harm, at times their presence was disturbing and upsetting. Ruth recalls seeing some strange eyes peering into her bedroom window. She had a system of classifying these "friendly intruders." If they barged right into the yard, usually they were from the Baptist campground near Ridgecrest. If they simply stopped for a quick look, they were most likely southern Presbyterians. Only the Episcopalians drove past the house at a discreet pace.

One day when their daughter Bunny was about three or four, Ruth noticed that her little red purse had more coins than her weekly allowance. She commented about it to Beatrice Long, who had begun helping Ruth around the house. Beatrice suggested that Ruth watch the next time tourists arrived at the house. So Ruth watched, and to her absolute surprise and amazement, she saw Bunny walk up to the gate with her little red purse over her arm. She smiled at the people and held out her purse. The tourists inevitably slipped her some coins. Ruth quickly put an end to Bunny's little game, but the situation showed how the Graham family was really living in a fish bowl.

Billy had a study with a large window, which was on the ground floor of the house and level with the road. Sometimes he crawled on all fours from his desk to the door to escape the eyes of curious onlookers.

Ruth was deeply troubled that Billy's call to preach had somehow made the Graham home public property. And Billy wrestled with the need to be away from his young family for weeks on end. Both Grahams were determined to keep their children away from the public eye, and especially the media. They certainly didn't want to put their children on display at the crusades. They were normal kids, and they wanted to keep them that way.

With the family's growing need for privacy, Billy learned about a sizeable piece of property up the mountain. A Jeep was about the only way to travel the rough road to reach it. Most of the area was covered with pine, poplar, and oak. In 1954, the Grahams purchased a large tract of the property for about thirteen dollars per acre. The site they settled on for the new house was about a mile straight up as the crow flies from Montreat. The surveyors had difficulty marking the property because of the rough terrain, but finally called it two hundred acres.

At first, it was difficult to choose the right spot to put the house, even though there were only a few possibilities. Finally, they decided on an area with a magnificent view and a spring that never went dry.

E. O. Spencer, a hotel magnate from Jackson, Mississippi, whom Billy had befriended, recommended that they hire an architect to at least look over the site. They thought the suggestion was a good one because of the steepness of the property and the potential for unstable ground.

Spencer's friend Joe Ware, his own architect, came from Mississippi to Montreat and looked over the place where the builders had already cut into the mountain to make a ledge for the home. In no uncertain terms, Joe said it would be necessary to put down pilings into the bedrock. So the builder obliged and put pilings into the ground before he poured the concrete slab for the foundation. It was good to have expert advice early on.

As the Grahams gathered materials to start building their home, Ruth's romantic sense of history came into play. She scoured the mountain communities and purchased old timbers from abandoned log cabins and bricks from an old schoolhouse. As construction developed, it took on the look of a century-old dwelling, even down to the split-rail fences. Inside, Ruth designed an informal country-home atmosphere that crossed the spans of time. She filled it with antiques that she picked up at auctions, junk shops, and secondhand stores.

The Grahams built most of the home in 1956, which was the year that Billy went to India for a series of crusades. Ruth loved fireplaces, and before Billy left, he conceded to her having two. When he was gone, Ruth told the workmen, "Build fireplaces! Build them faster than you ever have in your life! I want five before he gets back." The workmen managed to pull it off, and she always felt a bit of divine judgment that the fireplace in Billy's quarters smoked!

Chapter 10

MINISTRY OVERSEAS

I n the spring of 1954, Billy faced the greatest test of his young ministry. The greater London crusade was scheduled for three months—March through May. The evangelist's ministry outside the United States was not yet well established and he was tense. He insisted that Ruth accompany him. Uneasy about leaving her four children (Gigi, Anne, Bunny, and Franklin) for such a long time, Ruth agreed to go if she could return home after one month. During the meetings, her plans changed, and she stayed the entire time—the longest span away from her children for their entire lives.

If the press helped establish Graham as a national figure with the 1949 Los Angeles crusade, the London crusade had the opposite effect—at least at first. The trauma with the press began when the BGEA office in Minneapolis printed a calendar about the London crusade and sent it to people who were interested in their work. One word in the calendar was mysteriously changed, and the error brought the wrath of the British press and the Labour Party (which was socialist in its philosophy). Billy's remark was, "I could not blame them."

The statement read, "What Hitler's bombs could not do, socialism [which had been substituted for Billy's word *secularism*] with its accompanying evils shortly accomplished." The mistake was discovered and corrected before many were distributed, but one of the copies reached London and the hands of one newspaperman and a member of parliament.

The press continued to harass Graham throughout the crusade, but gradually after interviews and press conferences, the journalists acknowledged the American evangelist had skill and patience in answering their tricky and antagonistic questions.

The London crusade was held in Harringay Arena and lasted three months of nightly meetings. In the long history of this 12,000-seat arena, no speaker had ever filled it for more than one night. The BGEA executive committee had never seen such an outpouring of faith.

On opening night, the London dailies sent a horde of photographers and reporters, which included theater and literary critics as well as foreign and industrial correspondents. The weather was foul and worse than usual. The meeting was scheduled to begin at seven in the evening, and the steady rain had turned to sleet.

At six-thirty, Ruth and Billy were climbing into their car to drive to the arena when they received a message that not more than two thousand people were in their seats, and the crowd looked small in such a mammoth place. More than three hundred members of the press were watching. The Grahams held hands in silence as they drove to the arena. Billy thought about the gloating stories that the news reporters would write, but also about the prayers from around the world for that night.

Billy turned to Ruth and said, "Honey, let's just go and face it and believe God has a purpose in it."

As they reached the door, Billy heard the news, "The arena is jammed."

"What do you mean, jammed?" he asked. "We didn't see anybody as we approached."

"The main entrance is on the other side. Most of the traffic and people came from that direction. The place is full and running over, and hundreds are waiting outside."

As the Grahams made their eight-mile journey to the arena, thousands of people poured out of the underground trains and filled the seats. Tears welled up in the Billy and Ruth's eyes in gratefulness to God when they saw the throng of people hungry for the Word of God.

Billy reported to his ministry back home in America, "At the end of the first week, our arena was jammed an hour before meeting time, and the police reported that thirty thousand had failed to get in. By the end of the first month, Londoners were almost fighting for free tickets. Socialites came to see and to hear and to be converted. Bishops were willing to sit with us on the platform. Even newspapers became friendly."

Because many people traveled long distances to the arena, yet were unable to get into the building, the team began to use landline relays (live broadcasts by telephone lines). A total of 405 halls and churches carried the message successfully to many parts of the British Isles.

One night Charlie Riggs was supervising the landline relay meetings in a crime-ridden area of South London. A gang of tough youths arrived outside determined to break up the meeting. A broad-shouldered Christian police officer named Tony stopped them, saying, "You fellows are a bunch of cowards. If not, you would accept Christ as your Savior."

"*You're* not a Christian, are you?" one of the youth exclaimed in disbelief. "I've never heard of a Christian copper. How'd you get to be that way?"

Tony leaned against the wall and told the young people how Christ had saved him and changed his life.

One of the youth stepped forward and asked, "What do you have to do to become a Christian?"

In straightforward language, Tony told him how to accept Christ, and then included a warning that it would take courage.

"I've got courage, and I'd like to become a Christian," the youth replied. While his fellow gang members watched, Tony led the young man into the theater as the invitation was being given.

During this marathon of meetings, Billy had to prepare new messages continuously. Of the seventy-two addresses that he preached in the evenings, at least fifty were prepared on the day they were delivered. Early in the morning and late at night, the evangelist studied and wrote his outline; then he dictated the message, and his assistant typed up the notes. Often he received the final draft just before he stepped into the pulpit. He felt the presence and power of the Holy Spirit in preparing those talks, and when he stood up, he increasingly felt a greater power from the Lord, which never failed to refresh him.

The final meetings were scheduled in two of the largest arenas in London—White City and Wembley—with both meetings the same afternoon. Billy preached to about two hundred thousand people, certainly the largest religious gathering in British history. Over a period of three months, more than two million Britons heard Graham preach, and more than thirty-eight thousand decisions were made for Christ.

The team was preparing to leave for a brief vacation in Scotland. That morning, Billy received an unexpected call from the assistant to Prime Minister Winston Churchill. "Would you be available," he asked, "to join Mr. Churchill for lunch here tomorrow noon?"

The exhausted evangelist said, "I'm honored, but it would be impossible. We are leaving this evening for Scotland." Later, Billy remarked that his exhaustion showed in his turning down such an invitation.

Half an hour later the phone rang again. "Would you be able to meet with Mr. Churchill at noon today? He has a lunch scheduled at twelve-thirty with the Duke of Windsor, who is flying over from Paris, but he can see you before that."

From the assistant's own writings, Billy much later learned that Churchill had been nervous to meet him and paced the room asking, "What do you talk about to an evangelist?"

When Billy arrived at 10 Downing Street, the assistant discreetly reminded him that the prime minister had exactly twenty minutes. He was shown into a dimly lit cabinet room where Mr. Churchill stood and shook his hand. The tall American towered over the short dignitary. Churchill motioned for Billy to sit in the chair beside him. There was no one else in the room.

"Well, first, I want to congratulate you for these huge crowds you've been drawing," Churchill began.

"It's God's doing, believe me," Billy said.

Squinting at Graham, Churchill said, "That may be, but I daresay that if I brought Marilyn Monroe over here, and she and I together went to Wembley, we couldn't fill it."

Billy laughed, trying to imagine the scene.

"Tell me, Reverend Graham, what is it that filled Harringay night after night?"

"I think it's the Gospel of Christ," Graham said without hesitation. "People are hungry to hear a word straight from the Bible. Almost all the clergy of this country used to preach it faithfully, but I believe they've gotten away from it."

"Yes," Churchill said with a heavy sigh. "Things have changed. Look at these newspapers; they're filled with nothing but murder and war and what the Communists are up to. You know, the world may one day be taken over by Communists."

Billy agreed with him, but didn't comment and merely nodded.

Churchill continued. "I'll tell you, I have no hope. I see no hope for the world."

"Things do look dark," Graham agreed. They talked at length about the world situation.

Then the prime minister looked at him and said, "I am a man without hope. Do you have any real hope?"

"Do you mean you are without any hope for your soul's salvation?"

Churchill replied, "Frankly, I think about it a great deal."

Turning to his New Testament, Billy briefly explained the way of salvation. He was simple and direct, and he watched for any sign of offense—none was offered, and the prime minister seemed receptive.

At precisely twelve thirty, the assistant knocked on the door and announced, "Sir Winston, the Duke of Windsor is here for your luncheon."

"Let him wait!" the prime minister growled and waved him off. Turning back to Billy, he said, "Go ahead."

The evangelist continued talking for another fifteen minutes, then asked if he could pray for the prime minister.

"Most certainly," he said as he stood. "I'd appreciate it."

Billy prayed for the difficult situation the prime minister faced and for the world in general. Then he verbalized again that God was the only hope.

Mr. Churchill thanked Billy as he walked to the door. When they shook hands, he leaned forward and asked, "Our conversations are private, aren't they?"

"Yes, sir," Graham said in accordance with his policy never to quote a private conversation with a leader during that person's lifetime.

Each crusade opened up more opportunities and more requests for the Graham team to come to another part of the world. Before the London meetings, Bob Evans, a friend of Billy's from his Wheaton College days who founded Greater Europe Mission, set up a series of fairly modest one-day rallies across the European continent. The publicity from London changed the situation, so they moved the meetings to the largest arenas in each city. The team went from Helsinki to Stockholm to Copenhagen to Amsterdam to Berlin to Paris. In each place, lives were touched for Christ, and the Good News of Jesus was proclaimed.

In Helsinki, the team had the strong support of the Lutheran bishop, even though the state-supported Lutheran Church wasn't officially involved. The first evening had an overflow crowd. The second evening was estimated to be thirty thousand, the largest crowd in Finland gathered for a religious event. That evening, George Beverly Shea sang his beloved song, "I'd Rather Have Jesus" in Finnish. A local pastor wrote out the language phonetically so he could sing it. The attempt was so successful that it initiated the practice of singing at least one song in the native language of the host country, a practice that has been used almost without exception in the BGEA international crusades.

During this particular tour of Europe, the team went to Germany for a series of meetings. In Dusseldorf, they held a public service for the first time for an all-German audience. Some thirty-four thousand people filled the Rhine Stadium. The local committee had been skeptical that anyone would respond to the message and so had not trained local counselors and ushers. After the invitation was given, some Christian airmen from the nearby U.S. base were recruited to direct people to the tent for inquirers. Twice as many people came for counseling as the tent could accommodate.

About midnight Billy and the team returned to their hotel rooms. Two hours later, Graham called Bob Evans and Jerry Beavan to ask for help. They came immediately and found Billy writhing in agony on the bathroom floor. He was unsure if he had been poisoned or what the problem was. Through recommendation of John Bolten (the German-born industrialist), they called a local doctor, who turned out to be a Christian and had attended the meeting in Dusseldorf. He gave Billy a painkilling shot, and they got him to a specialist in the morning.

The doctor's X-rays showed a kidney stone, and they insisted Billy enter the hospital for a complete physical. However, the next meeting on the schedule was the largest one planned; it would be held in Berlin's Olympic Stadium where a decade earlier, Adolf Hitler had inflamed the minds and hearts of his followers. Billy said, "I'm determined to preach in Berlin, even if they have to carry me out on a stretcher."

From that moment on, the evangelist refused to take any more painkillers. He didn't want to be groggy when he preached in Berlin.

That night, as John Bolten sat by his bedside, Billy asked, "Why is God doing this to me? Or is it Satan? I can't understand it!"

As the men talked, it occurred to Billy that God was humbling him and increasing his dependence on the Lord. God alone would receive glory. The dangers of depending on his natural strength were very real. He read from the prophet Isaiah, "For mine own sake, even for mine own sake, will I do it…and I will not give my glory unto another" (Isaiah 48:11 KJV).

Despite a steady rain, eighty thousand people poured into the stadium, a record for any postwar event. The *Manchester Dispatch* said, "There has been no such crowd since the days of Hitler." The offering contained a large amount of East German currency, and the team speculated that as many as twenty thousand had come from the communist Eastern Zone (the Berlin Wall had not yet been erected).

The evangelist began his message with an allusion to Hitler's use of the same stadium: "Others have stood here and spoken to you." Then he raised the Bible. "Now God speaks to you." Then he retold Jesus's story of the rich young ruler in Mark 10.

Stadium regulations did not allow people to come forward to the platform. But five days later, when the team was on a ship in the Atlantic and headed home, they received a radio phone message from Berlin saying that sixteen thousand Germans had filled out decision cards. The Berlin committee organized a series of meetings to help those who made decisions understand their commitment. Later, they discovered that many people were unclear about what it meant to turn their lives over to Christ. The idea of making a personal decision to follow Christ was new to these Germans, possibly because of their background in the Lutheran state church. Through the follow-up process, many came to understand the meaning of salvation and made a full commitment to Christ.

Less than a year later, the BGEA team returned to Scotland for six weeks of meetings. Greater than any previous crusade, the meetings in Glasgow attracted large numbers of unchurched people, in part from a new program called Operation Andrew. While the basic approach had been used in other crusades, Charlie Riggs and Lorne Sanny refined the concept in Glasgow. The name of the program came from the disciple Andrew in the New Testament, who brought his brother Peter to Christ. Individuals were encouraged to make a deliberate effort to pray for an unchurched or uncommitted friend and to bring that person to the meeting. Lorne and Charlie also revamped the process for recruiting and training counselors more effectively.

The response was far beyond anything the BGEA team could have imagined. Using telephone lines during Easter week from Kelvin Hall, the Scottish evangelist D. P. Thompson helped the team organize rallies in thirty-seven locations; over one thousand people later attended follow-up classes from these meetings. The crusade was not limited to Scotland. On Good Friday, the BBC aired on both TV and radio a special sermon that Billy Graham had prepared on the meaning of the Cross. The broadcast was said to reach the largest audience for a single program since the coronation of the queen. Later, the team learned that the queen watched the program.

Since his days studying anthropology as a student at Wheaton College, Billy had been fascinated with the subcontinent of India. Its population in 1956 was more than four hundred million. He had asked God to someday open the door for him to minister there.

In January 1956, the team made the eight-thousand-mile trip from New York to India. John Bolten joined the team for the journey. During a stopover in Athens, he talked with Billy about how the apostle Paul made the Gospel relevant to the people of Mars Hill (Acts 17).

John said, "Billy, you are on your way to India, a country that has no concept of God. You will need a special approach to break into people's thinking, because they know nothing of the Bible or of the living God. Do you have such an approach in mind?"

Graham admitted that he didn't and suggested that they make the issue a matter of concentrated prayer. After they took off from the next stopover in Cairo, they flew near Mount Sinai, where God had given the Ten Commandments to Moses. Suddenly, Billy knew the answer. Jesus had been born in the single part of the world where three great continents intersected—Asia, Africa, and Europe.

Everywhere he went, Billy included in his message, "I'm not here to tell you about an American or a Briton or a European. I am here to tell you about a Man who was born right here in your part of the world, in Asia. He was born at the place where Asia and Africa and Europe meet. He had skin that was darker than mine, and He came to show us that God loves all people. He loves the people of India, and He loves you."

The eyes of the audience lit with understanding when they realized that Christianity was not exclusive to Europeans or to the white race, but that Christ came for all.

The team traveled throughout India, and in each location, the evangelist reassured his audience that it was wrong to think of Christianity as a Western religion. In New Delhi, his interpreter into Hindustani was a scholar named Dr. Akbar

Abdul-Haqq. His father had walked throughout that part of India proclaiming Islam, but during a stint at a mission hospital for medical treatment, he forsook the Islamic priesthood and accepted Christ. His son, Dr. Abdul-Haqq, was a Methodist who earned his doctorate from Northwestern University in Chicago and was the head of the Henry Martyn School of Islamic Studies in Aligarh, India. He admitted to Billy that he wasn't very supportive of the crusade at first, and for two or three weeks, he turned down the request to interpret for Graham. But after the first night, when he observed firsthand the response of the Indian people to the biblical Gospel, he made a confession: "I believe God has called me tonight to be an evangelist."

Several months later, Dr. Abdul-Haqq joined the BGEA team as an associate evangelist and has had a great impact on many lives in his native India and throughout the world, especially in the universities.

After finishing in India, the team made a whirlwind preaching tour in other parts of Asia, including the Philippines, Hong Kong, Taiwan, Japan, and Korea.

In 1972, Dr. Graham and the team returned to India for another series of meetings. On this trip, Billy met a historical figure. At the Calcutta airport, the American consul met Dr. Graham. He was a friend of Mother Teresa, and took Billy to meet her in the home where she and her co-workers ministered to Calcutta's dying. In addition to her tremendous work, Billy was deeply touched by her humility and her Christian love. She mentioned that during the previous night she had held five people one-by-one as they died in her arms, and she told them about God and His love.

"Why do you do what you do?" Billy asked.

She quietly pointed to a crucifix on her wall.

From Calcutta, the team flew to Dimapur, and then drove three hours on a dusty road to reach Kohima in the remote area known as Nagaland. As they rounded the curve about three or four miles from the city, tens of thousands of people lined the road to greet them.

When they reached the soccer field where the meetings would be held, there were ninety thousand already inside, with thousands more standing outside. Each of seventeen different tribes had its own interpreter with a public address system. After Billy spoke each sentence, he paused for the interpreters and could hear the hum of a mixture of dialects.

Following the meeting, they went to a government house where they were to spend the night. The chief minister of the local cabinet had arranged a dinner for the team. After the meal, they discussed plans for the next day.

The chief minister said, "We have early-morning Bible studies. Of course, we would like you to preside, but because you have several other responsibilities during the day, if you want to send one of your associates, we'll accept that."

Billy replied, "Maybe Charlie or Cliff could take the meeting. How many do you expect?"

Without hesitation, the minister said, "About one hundred thousand."

"I believe I'll take the meeting after all," Billy said.

A little later the team was shown their quarters in the government house where they met Nihuli, the man who would handle their baggage and shoes, make their tea, or whatever else was needed. When he proceeded to clean the mud from their shoes, Billy protested.

"We can do that!"

"No, please let me," Nihuli said.

As he carefully brushed their shoes, Billy asked about some of the details for the Bible session the next morning. He especially wanted to know who would be teaching the Bible before he arrived. Nihuli was silent, so Billy pressed again. Finally, the young man admitted to Graham that he himself would be teaching the Bible to the huge crowd. The man cleaning Billy's shoes taught him a valuable lesson about the servant attitude and the spirit of ministering. He never forgot the experience.

When Billy went to bed that evening, he could already hear the crowd assembling and praying in the darkness. The next morning as he looked down from the platform, he saw a sea of people dressed in tribal attire. They wore many different colors on their faces and carried spears and guns in their hands. Some of them had traveled from as far away as Nepal and China, walking as long as two weeks to hear Billy Graham speak and to hear his words interpreted into as many as seventeen languages.

The time Billy spent in India was truly unforgettable. The impact of the Gospel spread to the subcontinent and throughout vast regions of Asia.

Chapter 11

THE LIFE-CHANGING IMPACT OF THE PRINTED PAGE

After the 1949 Los Angeles crusade, Billy understood the power of the media to inform the public of his evangelistic work. Beyond promotion, he wondered if mass media could be used directly for evangelism. Besides radio and films, Billy turned his attention to the printed page. After all, the impact of words on paper could be felt long after the temporary effects of radio or film.

A few months after the *Hour of Decision* radio program began in 1950, the *Chicago Tribute-New York News* syndicate asked Walter Bennett about the possibility of Billy Graham writing a daily syndicated column. This column would deal with everyday problems from the viewpoint of the Bible. After some discussion, Billy said that he would be willing to give it a try if they provided others to assist him, under his supervision, in the event he was unable to do it. They agreed as long as he or someone he trusted approved the contents of each column. "My Answer" was born, and it continues with a circulation of about twenty million readers.

At a crusade in Dallas in 1952, an editor from Doubleday heard his messages and thought they might be turned into a book. Graham worked on the project off and on for the better part of a year. He dictated the first draft in about ten days using an Ediphone, a machine that used bulky wax cylinders to record the message. He wrote the book under the conviction that God could use it to present the Gospel message in a simple but comprehensive manner to people who had little or no religious background. A few people gave him suggestions for the manuscript, and it was in the publisher's hands by August 1953. The book, titled *Peace with God*, was an immediate bestseller. It has sold millions of copies and been translated into fifty languages.

In the wee hours of a morning in 1953, Billy awoke with an idea racing through his head. He thought of a concept to reach a broader audience than that of the only Christian magazine available at the time, *The Christian Century*. Graham slipped out of bed and went upstairs to his study to write. A couple of hours later, he had completed a concept for a new magazine that he called *Christianity Today*. On paper, Billy described the various departments of the magazine, outlined editorial policies, and even estimated a budget. He wrote everything that he could think of about the magazine's organization and purpose. The publication would be based in Washington,

DC, and would have the best news coverage of any religious publication. Primarily, the magazine would be aimed at the clergy in the hope of restoring intellectual respectability and spiritual impact to evangelical Christianity. In a relatively short time, the magazine became a reality.

The first person Billy told about the publication was his father-in-law, Dr. Nelson Bell. To Graham's amazement, Dr. Bell had a similar idea for a magazine, which had often occurred to him. He became a key person in developing *Christianity Today*. One of the first actions he took was to bounce the idea off various ministers and professors. The reaction to it was overwhelmingly positive.

Eventually Billy and Dr. Bell shared the vision for this magazine with J. Howard Pew, the chairman of the board of directors for the Sun Oil Company. Early on in his relationship with this businessman, Billy had mentioned that they were thinking of starting a magazine. Now, the evangelist asked him boldly, "Would you contribute heavily to it?"

As Pew puffed on his cigar, he said, "I'll talk to my sisters about it. I think we can do it."

In the magazine's earliest years, Pew and his family generously supported *Christianity Today*. Billy says that without Pew's support the project would have failed. Dr. Bell gave up his successful medical practice in Asheville, North Carolina, and traveled regularly to Washington, D.C, to be the executive editor of the magazine.

The hallmark distinguishing *Christianity Today* was a commitment to the trustworthiness of Scripture as the Word of God. The publication also attempted to convey its message with love rather than to vilify, criticize, or beat down. Graham's vision was that the magazine would be pro-church and pro-denomination, and would become the rallying point of evangelicals within and without the large denominations.

On October 10, 1956, Billy Graham was staying in Louisville, Kentucky, at the Brown Hotel during a crusade when he received an airmail letter from Dr. Bell. It said, "My dear Bill, 285,000 copies of the first issue of *Christianity Today* finished rolling off the presses in Dayton at two a.m. today."

The lead editorial, entitled, "Why *Christianity Today*?" set the tone for what the magazine attempted to accomplish: "*Christianity Today* has its origin in a deep-felt desire to express historical Christianity to the present generation. Neglected, slighted, misrepresented—evangelical Christianity needs a clear voice to speak with conviction and love and to state its true position and relevance to the world crisis. A generation has grown up unaware of the basic truths of the Christian faith taught in the Scriptures and expressed in the creeds of the historical evangelical churches.... *Christianity Today* is confident that the answer to the theological confusion existing in the world is found in Christ and the Scriptures."

The initial reactions thrilled Billy Graham. A Lutheran minister in New York City told a conference that after reading the magazine, he got down on his knees and rededicated his life to God. A young Baptist minister told a denominational gathering that the article on the authority of the Bible in evangelism caused him to get on his knees before the Lord and rededicate his life.

Soon after the magazine was launched, Billy visited a Catholic theological school. He noticed a stack of *Christianity Today* magazines, which had been sent to the school free of charge.

He asked the man who was showing him around the school, "Is that magazine read and studied by the students much?"

"More than any other," the man replied.

In subsequent years, the publication moved from Washington, DC, to Carol Stream, Illinois, where it merged with a few other excellent publications. It continues to be one of the best managed in the publishing industry—secular or religious.

Before *Christianity Today* came into existence, Bob Pierce, founder of World Vision, mentioned to Billy Graham that they had started a magazine to tell their supporters about their work and to encourage them to pray. "It's almost doubled our income," he told Billy, adding that when people are informed regularly about an organization's work, the likelihood of their support in gifts and prayers is increased. Bob told Billy that something like this would help his work as well.

Graham's primary intent for the magazine was to publish evangelistic and devotional articles—not to raise financial support. There were some good publications from the evangelical perspective, and producing such a magazine seemed beyond the resources of the young organization. George Wilson, the Minneapolis office business manager, opposed the idea, saying that a periodical would require a new staff with journalism skills and a strong financial commitment.

But even as the plans developed for *Christianity Today*, Billy felt the need for two publications. *Christianity Today* would be intellectual and reach the clergy and lay leaders, while a second one would be a more popular publication geared to reach ordinary Christians and to help them with their evangelistic witness and daily Christian living. Graham wanted the second magazine to include some stories of conversions, simple Bible studies, devotional messages, and news of the crusades.

In April 1958, the BGEA team was in San Francisco for a seven-week crusade at the Cow Palace. Sherwood Wirt, a local Presbyterian pastor who had been a professional journalist, had an assignment from *Christianity Today* to cover the meetings. Woody, as his associates called him, was at one time a liberal theologian, but several years earlier had become a conservative evangelical. He held a PhD from the University of Edinburgh and had experience as a military chaplain as well as ministering to university students. Billy thought Woody's writing skills and quiet spirit were impressive, so he asked Woody to become the first editor of a second BGEA magazine. They debated various titles, including *World Evangelism*, and George Wilson suggested the name that was adopted: *Decision*. The magazine began with the November 1960 issue and had a print run of 299,000 copies. Today, the circulation is about 400,000.

In the first issue, Billy Graham described the mission of the magazine, which continues today: "The basic purpose of this magazine will be twofold: To provide spiritual food for Christians, and to publish evangelistic messages and articles aimed at reaching the secular mind and winning the nonbeliever to Christ."

The response to *Decision* convinced the Graham team that it met a need in many people's lives. Not only does it go to individuals around the world, but over the years, bulk copies have also gone to overseas missions groups, prisons, and hospitals.

Decision often has been used in unexpected and unusual ways. For example, some people have used their copies as wrapping paper for gifts sent to countries that are restrictive or closed to the Gospel. Unsuspecting customs officials apparently have never caught on to the reason for the distinctive wrapping paper.

One day, a well-dressed businessman came into the BGEA office in London. He told the manager, Maurice Rowlandson, that he had been an officer in a bank until alcohol ruined his life. He lost his job and family and eventually lived as a homeless man on the streets of London. One day, he was rummaging through a trash barrel looking for something to eat when he came across a crumpled copy of *Decision*. The cover story caught his eye, and he read the entire magazine. As a result, he turned his life over to Christ. Now, a year later, he was telling Maurice how he had reconciled with his family and was again working at the bank.

The printed page changes lives, and this experience has been repeated through the years as a direct result of the various publications from the pen of Billy Graham and his team.

Chapter 12

MIRACLES IN MANHATTAN AND BEYOND

I n the summer of 1955, Billy Graham and Grady Wilson were taking a break from the Paris crusade and playing a round of golf. Billy received a telegram at the golf club from George Champion, vice president of Chase Manhattan Bank, who headed the evangelism department of the Protestant Council of New York.

New York presented unusual challenges to evangelism. In a message to his supporters, Billy Graham wrote, "Humanly speaking, New York is the most unlikely city in the Western Hemisphere for successful evangelism." Part of the challenge came from the incredible diversity: about sixty ethnic groups—more Irish than in Dublin, more Italians than in Rome, more Germans than in Berlin, and more Puerto Ricans than in San

Juan. Also, at least one of every ten Jews in the world lived in New York City. According to the BGEA findings before the crusade, 58 percent of New Yorkers claimed no religious identity. Protestants were a distinct minority and made up only 7.5 percent of the population, and many of them were only nominally committed to the Christian faith.

Everything that happened in New York touched the world. The city was the business, financial, communications, and entertainment hub of the world. Billy believed that if New York could be reached with the Good News of Jesus Christ, then the effects would be felt in many other cities.

Quite unexpectedly, they were able to get an option on Madison Square Garden for the summer months of 1957. The crusade was scheduled to begin on May 15 and conclude six weeks later on June 30.

Billy spent a great deal of time before the New York crusade in spiritual preparation—prayer, reading the Scriptures, and talking with Ruth and members of his team about the task ahead of them. The fact that millions of people around the world were already praying for the crusade meetings gave Billy a great deal of reassurance in spite of any uncertainties they faced.

He wrote in his diary, "There are many of my friends who have predicted that the New York crusade could end in failure. From the human viewpoint and by human evaluation, it may be a flop. However, I am convinced in answer to the prayers of millions that in the sight of God and by heaven's evaluation, it will not be a failure. God will have His way. I have prayed more over this assignment and wept more over the city of New

York than any other city we have ever visited. Now it is in God's hands."

The press was asking Billy and the others in BGEA for interviews before the event. Then, when Graham came to the city, the media intensity increased. Arriving at their hotel, the Grahams found a score of reporters patiently waiting for them. Ruth wrote in her diary, "There is a notable difference in the press from what it used to be. They are more respectful, friendlier. It may not last or it may—but thank God for it, while it lasts."

Walter Cronkite, for the CBS television news show, interviewed Billy, and with some hesitation, Billy appeared on *The Steve Allen Show,* wondering if he had any business appearing on an entertainment variety program. Ruth Graham, a private person, struggled with the media attention, but together, they realized the importance of it and learned to live with it. Billy wrote in his diary, "It is strange how one has gotten used to publicity. I used to so terribly resent the invasion of privacy; now we have learned to live with it and have dedicated it many times to the Lord. I realize that the same press that has made us known could ruin us overnight."

The first meeting in Madison Square Garden remains a ministry highlight for Billy Graham. He could see that the 19,500-seat arena was filled. Cliff Barrows directed a 1,500-voice choir, and Beverly Shea was in top singing form.

After the evangelist greeted the audience, he said, "We have not come to put on a show or to entertain. We believe that there are many people here tonight who have hungry hearts. All your life you've been searching for peace, joy, happiness, and forgiveness. I want to tell you, before you leave Madison Square Garden this night of May 15, you can find everything that you have been searching for in Christ. He can bring that inward, deep peace to your soul. He can forgive every sin you've ever committed.... Forget me as the speaker. Listen only to the message that God would have you retain from what is to be said tonight." After he spoke from the first chapter of Isaiah, 704 people came forward and made decisions for Jesus.

The following morning, the *New York Times* covered the opening service with three full pages and reprinted every word of the sermon. Most of the other five daily newspapers gave the crusade extensive coverage, and most of the regular columnists wrote about the meeting. The attendance continued to build each night.

On Saturday, June 1, the crusade was aired live on ABC, setting a new precedent for the BGEA. The program was up against two of the most popular programs on television, *The Perry Como Show* and *The Jackie Gleason Show*. A few days later, when the Trendex rating returned, the television officials were surprised—the *Herald Tribune* reported the program "provided the ABC network with its highest rating to date for the time period opposing the Como and Gleason shows."

A few years earlier, Grady Wilson became the first associate evangelist. Then in 1955, they added two others, Leighton Ford, brother-in-law to Billy Graham, and an Englishman, Joe Blinco. Initially the associate evangelists were to help Billy with his meetings and to take auxiliary meetings. Eventually, the associate evangelists began holding their own crusades when none of Billy's events were scheduled.

The greatest use of associate evangelists was the New York crusade in 1957 where there were about a dozen full-time associate evangelists and some who just came to help in that crusade. Because this crusade spanned a number of weeks and covered a vast metropolitan area, these men formed a vital part of the team.

At this event, Leighton Ford was in charge of setting up the meetings for the associate evangelists. One day, Howard Butt from Texas came into the office where they were booking meetings. He took a deep breath and said, "I have one hour today when Leighton hasn't booked some place for me to go."

There were luncheon and breakfast meetings as well as visits to schools and prisons. The associate evangelists also conducted individual counseling sessions, and the majority of these meetings were held during the day with the crusade being the focus of the evening meetings.

During the New York crusade, a television program was broadcast every night at 11:00 p.m., during which Leighton Ford, Joe Blinco, Grady Wilson, and other associates delivered a Gospel message.

An ABC executive was quoted saying, "The rating means that approximately 6.5 million viewers watched Dr. Graham, enough to fill Madison Square Garden to capacity every day for a whole year."

The team was receiving some ten thousand letters a day, and many of them were from ministers saying that new people were coming to their churches, and their attendance in July was higher than any previous period. During the telecasts, they spoke briefly about the need for money to continue, and from the very first, the contributions more than covered the costs.

Altogether, the crusade had fourteen live telecasts during the summer, and the crusade was extended. In the first week alone, they received about thirty-five thousand favorable letters, and many of these people made decisions for Christ in the comfort of their homes. A few days after the first telecast, Billy Graham wrote in his diary, "I've begun to feel that perhaps we are holding the Madison Square Garden meetings almost entirely so we could have this telecast. Madison Square Garden is a world-renowned stage from which to speak to America."

Originally, the crusade was scheduled to end on June 30, but with each meeting filled to capacity or beyond, the committee quickly added three more weeks. Yankee Stadium would be the site of the final rally on July 20.

Billy struggled with the decision to extend the meetings because he felt physically depleted after the first six weeks. Also, he had run out of sermons, and each night he had to prepare a new one. Some nights during the latter weeks, he sat on the platform praying silently, "O God, you have to do it. I can't do it. I just *can't* do it." Yet each time he stood to walk to the podium, he felt the words come into his mind and heart. God gave him supernatural spiritual power.

For the final service in Yankee Stadium, a record crowd of 100,000 people attended with another 20,000 outside. The heat index was 93 degrees, and it was 105 on the platform. Vice President Nixon attended and sat on the platform with the BGEA team to extend greetings to the audience from President

Eisenhower. It marked the first time a national leader of such prominence attended a Graham crusade.

At this point, the crusade committee and the BGEA team had to make a decision about whether or not to extend the meetings. A few committee members thought the meetings should end, and felt that any venue other than Yankee Stadium would be anticlimactic. With his notation that hundreds were accepting Christ at each meeting, Dan Potter said to Charlie Riggs, "How can we stop when a new church is being born into the kingdom of God every night?"

Billy said, "The main points against continuing concern the climax and the danger to our reputation. Pentecost was a great climactic experience, but the followers of Jesus didn't stop until they were thrown out of the city. Calvary was the greatest climax in our history, but the Lord didn't stop there. As far as our reputation is concerned, that should not be a vital point. Christ made himself of no reputation." After a lengthy session of prayer, the committee voted to extend the meetings.

A few weeks later, Billy wrote to George Champion, saying, "I, too, had certain doubts about continuing…but in my period of prayer I could not get any peace about closing, even though I am sure the crowds will drop off…dramatically. Yet for some mysterious reason, I believe the Lord would have us carry on."

Billy's prediction with regard to the crowds wasn't accurate, because the crowds in the Garden continued almost without variance. When the next deadline for extension approached, the committee had almost no trouble deciding to extend as long as Madison Square Garden was available—which it was until Labor Day weekend.

What was accomplished in the weeks of meetings? Billy was the first to admit to the press that the sprawling city of New York seemed unchanged. But underneath the surface, many people were touched by those messages about the Cross of Christ. There was an endless list of dramatic conversions. One evening, a plainly dressed woman stood in the follow-up room with tears running down her cheeks as she asked Jesus Christ to come into her life. Her counselor asked her if she had anything to say, and she replied that she was afraid of her son: "He drinks a lot, and I'm afraid he might beat me when he finds out I've become a Christian." Before the counselor could get a word in, a voice nearby called out, "It's okay, Mom; I'm here, too."

The team heard about a man who attended a Madison Square Garden meeting and left unmoved. Some weeks later, he attended a rodeo in the same arena. As he was sitting there, the Holy Spirit reminded him of the crusade, and in the middle of the rodeo, he silently bowed his head and gave his life to Jesus Christ.

The Lord also used the crusade far beyond the single event. A seminary student named Michael Cassidy from South Africa stood in the inquiry room and was overwhelmed with what he was seeing. Silently he wondered if this type of event could happen elsewhere, and he sensed that God was saying yes. A few years later, Michael graduated from Fuller Theological Seminary and started an organization called African Enterprise to Reach Africa for Christ. The Lord has greatly used Cassidy as an evangelist to reach Africa.

The New York crusade also had a long-lasting impact on the Billy Graham Evangelistic Association. Through the television broadcasts, an estimated ninety-six million people had seen at least one of the meetings from Madison Square Garden. God was using television to open new doors, and it resulted in a flood of invitations to other major cities with broad sponsorship across denominational lines.

These meetings had a lasting personal impact on Billy Graham as well. He knew now that no city or area of the world—no matter how difficult on the surface—was closed to the Good News of Jesus through mass evangelism. The crusade took a toll on him physically. He lost at least twenty pounds and finished totally exhausted. In his later years, he felt that something during the New York crusade went out of him that he never fully recovered. After New York, the team never attempted any straight series of meetings of equal length. According to Billy Graham, evangelistic preaching is emotionally and physically draining because the evangelist is always pressing the crowd for a commitment, and this involves a battle with spiritual forces. The BGEA team returned several times to New York: in 1970 and 1990, and in 1991 for a one-day rally in Central Park, which drew a quarter of a million people—the largest audience Billy Graham has ever addressed in North America. In 2005, Mr. Graham held his final crusade in New York.

As the news of the first New York crusade spread, the BGEA team received invitations from cities across America and abroad that reached the one hundred mark. Overwhelmed with the need, the team could only ask for God's strength and wisdom to know where to go next. They went to Australia and New Zealand from February through July 1959, which marked the longest series of meetings ever held outside the United States.

Then starting in 1958, a new crusade pattern began to develop. The associate evangelist would go to the country or city and preach for a week or two before Billy arrived to speak for several days. This started in the Caribbean and was replicated in Africa and Australia, as well as in many other regions.

In 1959, the crusades in Australia spanned four and a half months and were held in every major city. Mr. Graham was in Melbourne and Sydney for extended periods. The associate evangelists preached in Perth and Brisbane, and Billy came in at the end of the meetings to share a brief message. These were very large meetings; the associate evangelists preached to crowds of 10,000 to 20,000 people every night.

Leighton Ford was sent from Sydney to a small city called Wagga Wagga. He preached at an evening rally on a cool night and got so hoarse that he almost lost his voice. Early the next morning Ford had to speak to new recruits at a training camp for the Royal Australia Air Force. The chaplain asked for an associate evangelist, so Leighton was sent to Wagga Wagga.

The 6:00 a.m. meeting was in the hangar, the worst place in the world for acoustics because of the steel and concrete. All of the young men sat on the floor. As Leighton started to speak, he tugged at the microphone and the cord broke. Without a public address system, he rasped through a brief message for three or four minutes and then had to quit. Leighton Ford felt disappointed and discouraged with the missed opportunity since it was likely that many of those young guys had never been to a church.

Ford returned to Sydney. The next week the air force chaplain came to Sydney and looked up Leighton. He said, "I want you to know that during the last week I've had at least twenty-five of those recruits come to my office. They wanted to know how they could know Jesus personally." Leighton prayed inwardly, *Lord, I thought You depended on my voice.*

In the years following the New York crusade, Billy Graham and his team held crusades in major U.S. cities: San Francisco, Sacramento, Charlotte, Indianapolis, Washington, Minneapolis, Philadelphia, and throughout the state of Florida. These meetings often lasted two to four weeks. When he wasn't speaking at meetings, Billy had engagements in many other locations including the annual Christmas services at West Point and Annapolis.

Then the team felt the Lord was moving them to turn south—the Caribbean, South America, and Mexico. At the same time, Billy knew that Protestants were in the minority in these places, and the Roman Catholic influence was strong. He also understood that while the relationship between Protestants and Catholics seemed cordial, in the rural areas of these countries, it sometimes turned violent.

Billy's goal with Catholics was not to preach against Catholic beliefs or to proselytize committed Christians within the Catholic Church. Instead, he simply proclaimed the Gospel to people who had never committed their lives to Jesus Christ.

Beginning in 1960, Billy Graham and his team turned their attention to Africa and held crusades in Liberia, Ghana,

Nigeria, the Congo, Rhodesia, Kenya, Ruanda-Urundi, Ethiopia, and Egypt.

During the many meetings on the African continent, Billy came away with an overwhelming impression that God was at work in Africa, and because of the movement for independence that was sweeping the continent, the conditions were ripe for an unparalleled spiritual awakening. He also gained a renewed determination to do whatever he could do as an evangelist to combat racism in his own country.

Back in the early 1960s, Billy asked Leighton Ford to the office in Montreat, North Carolina and suggested that he put together a team and a series of crusades across Canada. One of these crusades was held in an outdoor meeting on a hillside in Halifax, Nova Scotia, and Billy was scheduled to speak at the end. Mr. Graham arrived in Halifax a night early. He sat in the back of the crowd wearing a baseball cap and dark glasses so no one would recognize him.

Afterward he told Leighton that he noticed an older man who listened intently during Ford's preaching. When Leighton gave the invitation, this guy began to squirm. Billy figured the man was convicted of his need to accept Jesus. Mr. Graham leaned forward and tapped him on the shoulder. "Do you want to go forward and give your life to Christ tonight?" he asked.

The man turned around and stared at Billy for a minute then said, "Nah, I think I will wait until the big gun comes tomorrow night."

On a trip to South America in 1962, a photographer joined their staff for his first international trip. Russ Busby was a former portrait photographer who had done some work with the

Navigators. He would now be the team's official photographer. A majority of the official BGEA photos from crusades or any official event since that time have come from the camera of Russ Busby. At one stage in Busby's long career, President Johnson tried to lure him away to become the official White House photographer, but Russ turned down the offer, saying that he felt God had called him to the BGEA ministry.

One of the first stops in South America was Venezuela. After two evening meetings in Caracas, the team flew to Maracaibo for two more meetings. This area is the third-largest oil producing region in the world and a major source of Venezuela's wealth. In the city proper, they found a potentially explosive political situation with rising tensions between factions.

Dr. Graham addressed the state legislature, and then he was invited to a midday meeting in a nearby building. The man who invited him and the team appeared to be a Christian leader, and Billy agreed to go on the condition that he could present the Gospel. They entered a room with about fifty people, and a man with two pearl-handled pistols in his belt introduced Billy. As Dr. Graham stood to speak, he could see soldiers out front unloading guns from trucks. A few minutes into his remarks, a rock crashed through a window, and then he heard a shot or two. He and the others in front ducked under a table, and the man who introduced him said they should get out. The BGEA team stayed in the background, while their Venezuelan host sized things up in the hallway.

As they waited in the small room with the lights out, Billy suggested to Russ Busby, "Why don't you go out and get some pictures of what's happening? They might be some of the best pictures of your life."

Russ voiced his opposition to the idea. "No, thank you. They might be the *last* pictures of my life!"

Finally, their host appeared and told them to sneak out the side door into an alley. The evangelist and his team had no way of knowing whether it was a trap or not, but they followed his instructions. "If anyone starts shooting at you, stop. Don't move. They're very poor shots, and if you start moving, they might hit you!" When they reached the alley, the gunsmen had fled, so the BGEA team got into a car and left the area.

Later they learned that a violent demonstration had broken out. The room where Billy Graham had been speaking was riddled with bullets, and at least one man was wounded.

The rest of the trip to Latin America was without incident. The cumulative attendance totaled 250,000 with 9,000 decisions. Compared to some of the other numbers, these didn't seem large, but as Billy Graham told his listeners on *The Hour of Decision*, "I have never seen such spiritual hunger in all our travels around the world…. We learned once again that spiritual hunger is no respecter of person. It exists among the rich as well as the poor, and the truth of the Gospel appeals to men universally."

Between two crusades in South America in 1962, the first Chicago crusade was held in the new McCormick Place arena. Night after night, the arena was filled to capacity. Over a three-week period, 750,000 people attended, and there were some 16,500 decisions for Christ. The final rally attracted more than 100,000 people to Soldier Field on one of the hottest days of the year; the temperature soared past one hundred degrees. In fact, Billy cut his sermon short because of the heat.

Ironically, the short sermon had its consequences. The BGEA team was recording the sermon for later release on national television, and there was a seven-minute hole in the hour-long program. Billy returned to the empty stadium to speak for an additional seven minutes. On the surface, it appeared to be a technical disaster, but it turned out to be a dramatic conclusion to the program. The response was one of the highest the association has ever received from a television broadcast.

The evangelist would return to Chicago for other crusades and events in later years. In 1971, Mayor Richard J. Daley welcomed Billy Graham to McCormick Place and remained on the platform for the service. The crusade drew about thirty thousand young people.

After Beverly Shea sang the second hymn of the evening, Cliff Barrows led the large choir in a musical number. At that moment, a police officer rushed onstage and whispered in the mayor's ear, "They're coming."

Billy knew exactly who the officer was referring to. Some Satan worshipers had let it be known that they planned to storm the meeting and disrupt it. Now, this group was pouring down an aisle toward the podium, chanting as they came.

The mayor said, "Don't worry, Dr. Graham, my police force will handle it."

Throughout Dr. Graham's crusade ministry, the police had never needed to handle a disturbance in a meeting, and Dr. Graham didn't want this to be the first time. "Mr. Mayor," he said, "let me try another way first." He stepped confidently to the microphone and, interrupting the choir, announced, "There are three or four hundred Satan worshipers here tonight. They've said they are going to take over the platform. Now, I'm going to ask you Christian young people to do something. Surround them and love them and sing to them. Do not threaten them or hurt them. If you can, gradually move them toward the doors."

Hundreds of young people pointed their fingers toward heaven and began to surround the Satan worshipers with shouts of "God is love!" and then with songs, such as "Jesus Loves You." Gently they moved the disruptive force out of the arena.

Mayor Daley turned to Billy and said, "I ought to have you and your people control all the riots we're having around here!"

The next morning, one newspaper headline proclaimed, "Hell Raisers Are Routed By Jesus' Power."

Invitations flooded in to the BGEA from major cities all over the country, convincing Billy and the team that the New York crusade wasn't a single movement of God but something that would be repeated across America. He struggled to know where to go next.

Chapter 13

CONFIDANT AND PREACHER TO AMERICA'S PRESIDENTS

Throughout his evangelistic ministry, Billy Graham has moved the common person to make a commitment to Jesus Christ. He has also had an ongoing impact behind the scenes on every president from Harry Truman to Barack Obama. A few of the stories about Eisenhower appeared in chapter nine. Dr. Graham has been influential in the lives of other American presidents as well.

John F. Kennedy

Billy Graham had several opportunities to interact with the first Roman Catholic president of the United States, John F. Kennedy. Ten days before Kennedy's inauguration in January

1961, Dr. Graham was invited to Palm Beach, Florida, to spend a couple of days. After a round of golf, Billy rode back to the Kennedy house with the president-elect. On the way, Kennedy asked Billy, "Do you believe in the second coming of Jesus Christ?" The question came unexpectedly.

"I most certainly do," Billy said with resolve.

"Well, does my church believe in it?" Kennedy asked. "They don't preach it," he added. "They don't tell us much about it. I'd like to know what you think."

As they rode along, Dr. Graham explained how Jesus came to earth, died on the cross, and rose from the dead, and finally, Christ's promise to come back again. "Only then," Billy said, "will we have permanent world peace."

"Very interesting," Kennedy said, and he looked away. "We'll have to talk more about that someday." Then the conversation shifted and never returned to the subject.

After Kennedy became president, the Grahams saw the family on several occasions in the Oval Office and at other functions. The last time Dr. Graham was with President Kennedy was at the 1963 National Prayer Breakfast, and Dr. Graham had the flu.

"Mr. President, I don't want to give you this bug that I've got, so I'm not going to talk right to your face," Dr. Graham began.

"Oh, I don't mind," Kennedy said. "I talk with people all day long who have all kinds of bugs."

After Dr. Graham gave his short talk at the breakfast and President Kennedy gave his talk, the pair walked out of the hotel to the car in customary fashion. At the curb, the president turned to the evangelist and said, "Billy, could you ride back to the White House with me? I'd like to see you for a minute."

It was a cold, snowy day in Washington, and Dr. Graham was standing outside with the flu and without an overcoat. He said, "Mr. President, I've got a fever. Not only am I weak but I also don't want to give you this thing. Couldn't we wait and talk some other time?"

"Of course," the president answered graciously. The two men never talked about the matter, and it was the last time Dr. Graham saw President Kennedy before his ill-fated trip to Dallas in November 1963. The irrecoverable moment continues to haunt him, and he wonders what was on Kennedy's mind.

Lyndon B. Johnson

Billy Graham knelt many times at the bedside of President Lyndon Johnson. Billy saw incredible strength in this powerful personality from Texas. Dr. Graham once said of him, "Great men know when to bow."

While powerful, this longtime figure in Washington politics also knew how to be charming, coarse, and at times, profane. Whenever he swore in Billy Graham's presence, he would quickly turn and say, "Excuse me, Preacher."

The evangelist had known LBJ since he was a congressman. Now that Johnson was president, Billy tried to stop calling him by his first name. Occasionally, he slipped up, and the president gave Billy a funny look, which prompted him to correct himself.

On one occasion, Billy Graham and T.W. Wilson flew with President Johnson on Air Force One from Washington to

Atlanta, where the president was scheduled to speak to 30,000 schoolteachers and administrators.

Addressing the assembly, the president said, "Now, the reason I brought Billy Graham with me is because of the low ceiling at the airport. When I heard it was almost zero-zero, I thought I'd better have Billy with me."

Recalling the incident, Billy said, "We landed safely with a hundred-foot ceiling and a hundred-fifty-foot visibility. It was not to *my* credit, though. We all prayed."

One evening at the Johnson ranch outside Austin, the evangelist and the president sat in Johnson's convertible watching a beautiful sunset.

"Mr. President, have you ever personally received Jesus Christ as your Savior?"

"Well, Billy, I think I have," he said as he gazed out over the landscape.

Billy sat quietly in the car and waited for LBJ to continue.

"I did it as a boy at a revival meeting." Then, he paused and continued, "I did it reading one of the sermons in my great-grandfather's book of evangelistic sermons." Then, after another period of silence, he added, "I guess I've done it several times."

"When someone says that, Mr. President," Billy said carefully, "I don't feel too sure of it."

The president looked over at his friend with a puzzled expression.

"It's a once-for-all transaction," the evangelist said. "You receive Christ and He saves you. His Spirit bears witness with your spirit that you're a child of God."

LBJ nodded his head, and Billy didn't feel it was the time to say anything further.

Almost every time President Johnson and Dr. Graham parted company, President Johnson would make a request. "Preacher, pray for me." Then the Texan would drop to his knees for prayer—whether they were in the White House or the ranch house.

Richard M. Nixon

As with Lyndon Johnson, Billy Graham knew Richard Nixon from his days in Congress, then as vice president under Eisenhower. They had many occasions of interaction before Nixon became president of the United States, and that friendship carried over into the Nixon presidency.

Some nights President Nixon would call the Graham house in Montreat at one o'clock in the morning simply to talk. The essential bond between the two men was not political or intellectual but personal and spiritual. Less than two weeks before the 1968 election, Billy Graham was in New York and called Nixon when he came off the campaign trail to spend a day in his Fifth Avenue apartment. Dr. Graham invited him to attend a service at Calvary Baptist Church on West Fifty-Seventh Street. Pastor Stephen Olford preached a powerful evangelistic message entitled, "The Gospel in a Revolutionary Age."

The pastor pleaded for repentance and conversion on a personal and a national level. Afterward Nixon said, "The press go with me everywhere, and that was a great message for them to hear!"

Privately, Billy Graham urged President Nixon to be more forthright about expressing his spiritual convictions. And he wrote a reproving letter after President Nixon spoke at the 1974 National Prayer Breakfast. The letter appeared in Nixon's book *From: The President*. "While I know you have a personal and private commitment, yet at some point, many are hoping and praying that you will state it publicly…In taking such a stand you would find the deeper personal satisfaction in your own life."

While Graham had some personal misgivings about President Nixon's religious understanding, he never doubted the reality of the president's spiritual concern or his belief in Christ. Nixon told Billy, "I believe the Bible from cover to cover."

Gerald Ford

Gerald Ford was another president who spent years in Congress and was acquainted with Billy Graham before taking office. An outspoken Christian, Gerald Ford and Billy often interacted. Years after his presidency, Gerald Ford admitted to Dr. Graham that he initially questioned Graham's trip into Eastern Europe. He specifically criticized Billy Graham's trip to Romania, which had a poor record on human rights. Then the president watched one of the BGEA televised reports from Romania and saw the large crowds that had gathered to hear the Good News of Jesus Christ. President Ford changed his mind. After his presidency, he told an interviewer, "When I first read that Billy Graham was going to a Communist-dominated country, I had reservations. Yet there is no doubt…Graham reignited the flame of religious belief and conviction. And that, in turn, has unquestionably had a political impact on what is taking place."

Jimmy Carter

Billy Graham first knew of Jimmy Carter long before he ran for national office.

In 1966, the BGEA was using an evangelistic film for an outreach in Americus, Georgia. The film would be shown over several days, and the Graham Association insisted that the meetings be completely integrated. Racial integration wasn't common in rural Georgia, and they couldn't find a Christian leader to serve as the chairman of the outreach. At the last minute, a successful farmer and state senator from Plains, Georgia, stepped forward. It was Jimmy Carter.

None of the major churches would allow the group into their facility for the planning meetings. When the outreach began, Jimmy Carter stood night after night at the end of the film and invited people to come forward for spiritual counseling. Billy Graham didn't personally meet Carter during this experience, but he wrote him a thank-you note for his caring and daring assistance.

A few years later, in 1971, Jimmy Carter became the governor of Georgia, and he personally met Billy Graham. He willingly accepted Graham's invitation to serve as honorary chairman of the Atlanta crusade. Almost every night, Governor Carter attended the meetings to show his support for the event.

Billy Graham and President Carter had infrequent contact during his four years in office. One night, Ruth and Billy Graham were overnight guests of the Carters at the White

House. For several hours, the four of them talked about national affairs and their common southern backgrounds. The majority of the time, they shared their mutual faith in Jesus Christ and talked about issues that sometimes divide sincere Christians. At the close of the evening, the four of them prayed together and sensed a spirit of Christian love and oneness.

Ronald W. Reagan

Billy Graham met Ronald Reagan in 1953 when the future president was a strong Democrat. Reagan and Graham both spoke at a benefit to raise money for retired film stars. It was Dr. W. A. Criswell who caught Reagan's attention on that particular day. Dr. Criswell was the pastor of First Baptist Church in Dallas, which was the largest congregation of the denomination. He bluntly told Reagan that he had never seen a movie in his life, nor did he intend to ever see one. Then he added that the whole movie industry was of the devil.

Not one to back down from a challenge, Reagan explained how movies were made and pointed out that many of them had a wholesome message. After he heard Reagan's explanation, Dr. Criswell said, "I'm going to start seeing some movies. I'll even tell my congregation that it's not a sin to see certain types of movies."

Billy observed the exchange and saw that Ronald Reagan could not only change a man's mind but had the keen ability to use charm, conviction, and humor in the process.

After winning the presidential election in 1980, Reagan asked Billy Graham to join him in the inauguration ceremonies. He invited the evangelist to speak at the first official event of the day—a prayer service at St. John's Episcopal Church across from the White House—for the president-elect and the vice president-elect and their families.

About half an hour before the service, Billy Graham walked into St. John's. The only two people in the sanctuary were Frank Sinatra and his wife, Barbara.

Billy said, "Frank, I'll bet this is the first time you've ever been the first one in the church!"

Sinatra laughed and said, "I try to go as often as I can."

During the eight years of the Reagan administration, Billy Graham saw President Reagan a number of times. The president invited Billy and Ruth Graham to attend several state dinners for visiting foreign leaders.

One night in Washington, after Billy and Ruth had gone to bed at the Madison Hotel, the phone rang. It was First Lady Nancy Reagan.

"Are you asleep?" she asked.

"Just about," said Billy.

"We're in bed, too," Nancy said, "but we want to see you both and talk to you. Can you come over here?"

Billy agreed.

"We'll have a car in front of the hotel in fifteen minutes," Nancy said.

The Grahams dressed and rode over to the White House only to see the two chief occupants still in bed in their pajamas! The Reagans spent several hours talking with the Grahams about their families and personal concerns.

Billy often saw Reagan's spiritual side in the years before he was elected to public office. One time, Billy gave a small dinner party at the Beverly Hilton Hotel, and Reagan was invited. During their conversation, Reagan brought up the subject of the second coming of Christ. This same topic came up with President Reagan on several other occasions.

During his term, Reagan awarded Billy Graham the highest civilian honor the American government gives a citizen for service to the nation. Dr. Graham received the Presidential Medal of Freedom on February 23, 1983. The evangelist always appreciated his warm and enduring personal relationship with President Ronald Reagan.

George H. W. Bush

As with most previous presidents, Billy Graham knew George Bush before he became president. At the 1989 inauguration, George Bush invited Billy Graham to lead the various prayers of the public ceremony. Initially, Dr. Graham protested that it was customary to have clergy from different faiths, such as Jewish, Catholic, and perhaps Orthodox. The president-elect was firm with his plans, however, because he was more comfortable with Dr. Graham and also because he didn't want people to think he was playing politics by having representatives of different faiths.

After the inauguration, the Grahams were invited to attend a luncheon in the Capitol rotunda. Afterward, to their surprise, they were taken to the president's box at the reviewing stand to watch the inauguration parade. During a pause in the parade, the president motioned for Billy Graham to come to him, and then said, "Billy, would you and Ruth mind going back to the White House and seeing my mother? She's up there watching the parade, and I know she'd just love to have you with her."

Billy readily agreed to the request, and he and Ruth went to the White House. They found Mrs. Bush in frail health. She had been flown in for the event and was in the queen's bedroom, her face aglow.

After holding her hand for a few minutes, Billy asked if he could pray, and she nodded with a smile. He spoke a few words of thanksgiving, asking God to lead, guide, and protect George in the years ahead. After he had finished, he looked at Mrs. Bush, who, with tears in her eyes, said in a whisper, "He'll need it."

A short time later, Billy Graham called his longtime friend "Mr. President" instead of "George." The moment felt awkward, but President Bush understood that it was a dilemma for all of his other friends as well. The president stared into the distance, and at that moment, Billy Graham felt the loneliness and burden of the office of the president of the United States.

William Jefferson Clinton

Bill Clinton was the governor of Arkansas when he first met Billy Graham. Actually, Clinton had attended a Graham crusade at the age of eleven. It made such an impression on the young Clinton that he gave a portion of his allowance to the association.

As governor of Arkansas, Bill Clinton was the honorary chair of the Little Rock crusade. He and Hillary gave a luncheon for the Graham team and various leaders in the state. At the luncheon, Clinton asked a favor. "My pastor is dying of cancer. He lives several miles from here. I'd like to drive you to his home so that we can read the Bible to him, pray with him, and encourage him. He has meant a lot to me."

Asking further, Billy learned that Clinton's pastor was one of the leading pastors in the Southern Baptist Convention, Dr. W. O. Vaught, who played a key role in the crusade's coming to Little Rock. The governor drove Billy out to his pastor's house. When they walked into the bedroom, they were shocked to see how thin and frail Vaught looked, but he had an open Bible on his bed.

Billy spoke first. "W. O., we're certainly praying for you at this time that, if it is God's will, you will be healed."

"I have something for you, boys. Sit down," W.O. began, and then gave a Bible lesson that lasted about thirty or forty minutes. He finished with, "Now, let's have prayer. Let's each one of us pray. We'll pray for the crusade."

Governor Clinton and Billy Graham got down on their knees by the bed and prayed. When the governor and the evangelist left the house that day, they felt as though they had received far more encouragement than they had given to Clinton's pastor.

During Clinton's presidency, Billy Graham visited him on several occasions. One very significant time was when Ruth and Billy were presented with the Congressional Gold Medal on May 2, 1996, the highest honor the Congress of the United States can give to a citizen. The medal depicted Ruth and Billy Graham on one side and the new Ruth and Billy Graham Children's Health Center at Asheville Memorial Mission Hospital on the other side. Funds from the sale of the medal helped to provide health care for poor children across Appalachia.

After the award ceremony at the Capitol, President Clinton arrived at the dinner hosted by Memorial Mission Hospital. He spoke to the audience. "I hardly ever go to a place as president that Billy Graham hasn't been to before me, preaching." After his remarks, he presented Billy and Ruth with a framed copy of the legislative bill that authorized the Congressional Gold Medal, and the pen with which he had signed it. Afterward, they went backstage, and President Clinton gave Billy Graham a long hug before departing.

George Walker Bush

While President George W. Bush met with Billy Graham numerous times during his Presidency, one of his most significant exchanges occurred years before President Bush became president.

In the summer of 1985, President George H.W. Bush invited Billy to visit their family compound at Kennebunkport, Maine. The younger Bush recalled that while Billy was talking with some family members and answering their questions, "which was unbelievably exciting," as Bush put it, "my problem was I had about four beers and five wines. I was kind of listening to Billy through the haze of alcohol."

The next day Billy and George took a walk in the yard and started talking about religion. "I was obviously looking, yearning for something different with my life," George said. "Billy sent me a Bible, and I started reading it, but it took a while to fully understand that religion is not a course in self-improvement. Religion is surrender; you allow the living God into your life by surrendering to that living God." George W.

Bush says that encounter with Billy Graham moved him out of his alcoholism and into a relationship with Jesus Christ.

Later when George W. Bush was the governor of Texas, he sat behind Billy Graham during a crusade. "It was an unbelievable experience to see him give the invitation. He is not a magnet for Billy Graham but a magnet for a Higher Power."

After the September 11 tragedy in 2001, Billy Graham represented the Christian faith during the service at the National Cathedral. "He did a powerful job during that service," President Bush explained. "He will be a friend to every president because his mission is to preach the word—to the most powerful and the least powerful."

"When I was President, I was thankful that Billy came to the White House to visit. He has no political agenda. He just has an agenda of the Lord."

Barack Hussein Obama

In late April 2010, President Obama and First Lady Michelle took their daughters to one of their favorite vacation spots, the Grove Park Inn in Asheville, North Carolina. This picturesque resort is tucked away in the Blue Ridge Mountains. During the vacation, a senior staff member suggested the President might like to meet Billy Graham. The Graham home in Montreat is about half an hour away from the Grove Park Inn.

As they walked into the living room, they were unsure what to expect since at 91 Mr. Graham was limited in his health. As Billy sat in an old wooden chair, his body was hunched over but his mind was sharp. His first words to President Obama were, "I'm so proud of you!" Billy continued saying how he had followed the president's career for years and had been praying for him every day. Billy earnestly thanked the president for making the trip up the mountain to his home. It turned out President Obama was the first sitting president ever to visit Billy Graham in his home.

As their brief meeting drew to a close, Billy prayed for President Obama. Then as the prayer reached its conclusion, President Obama laid his hand on Billy Graham's knee and prayed for him. It was a powerful moment for the president and for the man who had been pastor to many presidents.

From Harry Truman to Barack Obama, Billy Graham has been an influential spiritual advisor to each president. Whether he has known them casually or intimately, Billy understands the burdens of the office of president of the United States and that the burden can't be carried with human strength alone but only through the spiritual power and strength God gives.

Chapter 14

TRAINING OTHERS IN EVANGELISM

B illy Graham traveled the world in the 1950s and beyond; he met many Christian leaders and noticed among them a lack of effective training in evangelism. As a partial answer to this need, the Billy Graham Evangelistic Association conducted three conferences for itinerant evangelists in 1983, 1986, and 2000 in Amsterdam. The conferences gathered evangelists from around the world into one place for training and inspiration.

These conferences marked the culmination of a dream of Dr. Graham's to help evangelists and to train them for the future. At one of the conferences, Billy and Ruth Graham walked into the dining room where several thousand people had gathered and were eating pre-packaged meals together. The Grahams sat with a man who appeared to come from a poor country. Billy asked, "Where are you from?"

"I am from Botswana."

Then, through some further gentle questioning, the African evangelist described traveling on foot from village to village to preach the Gospel to anyone who would listen. There was frequent opposition and little response.

Dr. Graham asked, "Are there many Christians in Botswana?"

"A few," the evangelist replied. "Only a few."

"What's your background? Did you go to a Bible school or get any education to help you?"

"Well, actually," the evangelist said, "I got my master's degree from Cambridge University."

Immediately, Billy Graham felt ashamed at having stereotyped the man, but he was also humbled to realize that any educated man returning to this part of the world could have virtually unlimited social position and power. However, the evangelist was completely at peace to follow Jesus Christ and to preach the Good News to his own people. He was one of 8,000 evangelists from 174 countries who attended the 1986 conference.

Some of Billy's motivation to train others came from the prodding of his BGEA staff, ones like Dr. Victor Nelson, the retired Presbyterian pastor who joined the team in the Minneapolis office and coordinated crusades in Canada for BGEA associate evangelists. Billy had a great deal of respect for the wisdom and counsel of Dr. Nelson.

One day, he came by Billy's hotel room in Nova Scotia, Canada, and said, "Billy, you just puddle-jump from crusade to crusade all over the world. You'll never accomplish what you could and should accomplish. You not only need to do this work yourself, but you need to multiply your efforts. You need to train others to do effective evangelistic work."

Billy knew the words of his trusted friend rang true, and there was a need to work toward an international conference on evangelism. Part of the challenge was that no network of evangelists existed in the world. After a great deal of prayer and research, the BGEA decided to sponsor the first International Conference for Itinerant Evangelists. The goal was to find 3,000 men and women who were involved in itinerant evangelism. They weren't sure where to find these evangelists, but they knew most of them would come from the developing world, which meant they would be unable to pay for the training because of their lack of personal property and the currency restrictions in their home countries.

The budget for this conference would have to be raised above and beyond the other evangelistic work of the association. One individual gave a large gift of $1 million for the conference, but most of the $9 million budget came from small donations, with the average gift being $15. They selected Amsterdam's RAI Center because it was one of the few places that could accommodate a large number of people, and Holland had few visa restrictions.

One of the biggest challenges of the conference was selecting the participants. The team began with a list of 1,000 names of men and women who were involved in evangelism, and as time went on, the list grew to more than ten thousand. They developed a process to review all the applications and to make sure the participants were actively involved in evangelism.

The proceedings were translated into ten different languages, and the group was a microcosm of the human race, the largest number coming from India, then Nigeria, then Brazil. Some of the delegates arrived barefoot and without a change of clothing. They were overwhelmed when they visited the clothing center provided for the conference. There were five hundred tons of clothing—shirts, pants, dresses, and children's wear, all distributed free of charge from Franklin Graham's organization, Samaritan's Purse.

The participants received a small library of free books in a canvas bag to help them prepare their messages and study the Bible for their evangelistic work. Also, more than two hundred workshops were given that dealt with everything from organizing a crusade to re   ˜˜˜ss and political leaders to studying the Bible.

A team of scholars
statement directed to t
the Amsterdam Affirm
of fifteen affirmation
Great Commission,
and ministry.

The last affirma
beseech the body of
for peace in our wo
the biblical priori

oneness of believers in Christ for the fulfillment of the Great Commission, until Christ returns."

At the end of the conference, each participant stood and read the affirmation, and then responded in his native tongue with the words, "This I affirm."

In his closing address, Dr. Graham said, "These itinerant evangelists are the most important ambassadors and messengers on earth. They are a mighty army of proclaimers, energized by the power of the Holy Spirit, spreading out across the world with a renewed vision to reach their own people for Christ."

The BGEA held a second conference three years later in 1986. The decision was not difficult, because their research had turned up the names of 50,000 men and women who were involved in itinerant evangelism. Eight thousand had been turned away from the first conference because of lack of space or financing.

In the year 2000, the Billy Graham Evangelistic Association held its third and largest international conference with more than 10,000 participants from 209 countries. The conference featured about three hundred plenary and teaching sessions. The speakers included some of the world's top Christian aders. All the major sessions were interpreted into twenty-anguages and broadcast on a low AM radio signal. With ls, the Amsterdam 2000 interpretation system st AM broadcasts ever run simultaneously in

easons, Billy Graham was unable to he addressed the gathering via among those who represent a generation of evangelists that hands the torch to a new generation of God's servants. We will go out from Amsterdam with a new fire burning in our hearts to touch a lost world."

The evangelism training hasn't only been at three major conferences. Every Billy Graham crusade trains counselors and lay leaders in evangelism and follow-up. Also, since 1967, the Billy Graham Evangelistic Association has been holding Schools of Evangelism in conjunction with the crusades and in other key locations around the world. To date, more than one hundred thousand pastors and Christian workers have attended a School of Evangelism. Though the School trained thousands of Christians, the events were expensive and limited by geography, including the time it took the students to travel to a live event.

In 2012, the Billy Graham Evangelistic Association launched a new online evangelism school aimed at pastors seeking to spread the Gospel and ordinary Christians looking to grow stronger in their faith. The four-session online course is available worldwide for only $99. The course is set up on a seminary level but is about understanding evangelism. Participants can study at their own pace, and they are given 180 days to complete the four courses. Each course contains transcripts of the audio and video recordings available for printing. It covers four topics—preparation, proclamation, power, and preservation. There are assignments and quizzes, and a certificate for each of the four sections. When they complete the course, they are awarded a diploma.

Bible training for the layperson takes place at The Cove, a conference center in North Carolina, and at the university level, evangelism training is given at the Billy Graham Center at Wheaton College.

These ongoing programs to train lay leaders in evangelism are only a few of the innovative ways that Billy Graham continues to pass on the legacy and lessons of his lifetime in crusade evangelism.

Chapter 15

PASSING THE BATON

Over the years, Dr. Graham has made regular trips to the Mayo Clinic in Rochester, Minnesota, for complete physical examinations. At the end of one visit, as Billy began to leave Dr. Dickson's office, the doctor asked him to sit back down and rise again. "Something looks not quite right about the way you're getting up out of the chair," he said.

Dr. Dickson made an appointment for Billy to see one of the Mayo neurological specialists. Following a battery of tests, the doctor pinpointed the problem—Parkinson's disease. No one in Billy's family history had the disease, and he knew little about it. Parkinson's is a progressive and incurable disease that slowly destroys the brain cells that deal with muscle control.

Ironically, the diagnosis came at a point when Dr. Graham was finding it increasingly difficult to travel to and preach at crusades. In recent years, the Mayo Clinic doctors have changed their diagnosis to say that Dr. Graham has a Parkinson's-like disease, which is controlled through a shunt implanted in his brain. Through regular visits to Mayo, the doctors monitor Dr. Graham's medication and control the disease.

During the 1990s, Franklin Graham, Billy's oldest son, began to hold crusades around the country as well as overseas. The bulk of Franklin's time was devoted to his two ministries, Samaritan's Purse and World Medical Mission. Operation Christmas Child, one of the ministries of Samaritan's Purse, is a popular program that provides Christmas gifts and Gospel literature to millions of children around the world. In late 2000, Franklin was named Chief Executive Officer of BGEA. The following year Franklin succeeded his father as president of the Billy Graham Evangelistic Association.

In 2005, from June 24th through the 26th, Billy Graham led his last crusade at Flushing Meadow-Corona Park, New York speaking to more than 230,000 people.

In 2006, Will Graham, the oldest son of Franklin Graham, held his first crusade-style event called Celebrations in 2006 in Leduc, Alberta, Canada. In 2012, Will held multi-day events in five countries across three different continents, including the United States, Canada, India, Australia, and Thailand. His 2013 schedule included Celebrations in Kenya, Japan, and Thailand. Currently, Will is a vice president and an associate evangelist of the Billy Graham Evangelistic Association as well as the executive director of the Billy Graham Training Center at The Cove.

On May 31, 2007, the Billy Graham Library was dedicated on the grounds of BGEA headquarters in Charlotte. The multi-story, 40,000 square foot exhibit tells the story of Billy Graham's life and ministry and makes an appeal for visitors to come to Jesus Christ as their Savior. Billy Graham's boyhood home was also moved onto the property and is open to visitors. Two weeks after the dedication, Ruth Bell Graham died. She was buried on the grounds of the library next to the site reserved for her husband.

In November 2013, BGEA launched "My Hope with Billy Graham," an evangelistic effort that culminated with the broadcast of Billy Graham's video message, "The Cross," in homes, churches, and on the Internet across two nations. More than 110,000 people made commitments to Jesus Christ through this program.

As Dr. Graham looks over his life and ministry, he says that he would study more, spend more time with his family, and speak less. Yet he has no doubt about the calling of God on his life and his commitment to reach every person in the world with the Good News of Jesus.

In February 1998, Dr. Graham appeared on *Larry King Live* with his longtime friend. In response to a conversation about death, Dr. Graham said, "I say that God has a plan for us all. I believe there is a moment right now that God has set aside when I am to die.... I may be shot. I have had all kinds of things in the past in different parts of the world, where people didn't like what I was preaching. And I think there is a moment when I'll die, and I am looking forward to it, actually, because I want to go to heaven."

From a life of faithful service to Christ and preaching the Gospel message all over the globe, Billy Graham is a living example of how God can powerfully use one person.

About the Author

W. Terry Whalin has always been fascinated with stories about people and their lives. As a youth, he read many biographies and later he wrote stories as a journalist. Terry has profiled more than 150 bestselling authors in more than fifty magazines including *Christianity Today* and *Writers Digest*. Terry is the author of more than sixty books including biographies of Chuck Colson, John Perkins, Sojourner Truth, Billy Sunday, Samuel Morris, and Luis Palau. An acquisitions editor at Morgan James Publishing, Terry and his wife Christine live in Colorado. His website is www.terrywhalin.com and his book website is www.BillyGrahamBio.com.